2 Close to Home

2 Close to Home

A Screenplay

Dean Andrade

www.DeanAndrade.com
AndradeDean@aol.com

To order additional copies of this book, contact:
Xlibris Corporation
1-888-795-4274
www.Xlibris.com
Orders@Xlibris.com
32709

Logline:

A cynical 33-year-old waitress butts heads with a moody
28-year-old actuary posing as a badass. The pair quickly
fall for each other amid explosions, gunplay, wisecracks and
criminal mischief. But a web of secrets threatens to blow
everything apart.

EXT. MIDWESTERN TOWN — DUSK

Traveling the outskirts of an aging rustbelt town, population
70,000, we see a vacant used car lot, houses with peeling
paint, an old factory with broken windows, the ruins of a
warehouse half demolished by a pair of idle bulldozers.
Then . . .

A dilapidated biker bar. A few cars and Harleys are lined up in
the dirt lot. A raccoon sniffs near a garbage bin, knocks off
the lid, then scurries away. The neon sign of the Circle J Bar
flickers to life, revealing a nest of twigs in the hook of the
J.

INT. CIRCLE J BAR — DUSK

The bar and its handful of patrons have seen better days.
Old license plates and taxidermy adorn the walls. Wisps of
cigarette smoke. Classic rock music. A stuffed black bear
stands guard near the door. He's wearing a pink bra.

A woman we will come to know as REBECCA shoots a game of pool
by herself. She's 33 years old, with pulled-back dirty blonde
hair and a trim muscular body. She's wearing ripped jeans and
a tight red T-shirt. After every shot she takes a sip from her
Pabst.

Nearby, a man we will come to know as BILL sits on a barstool,
lighting matches and flicking them into an ashtray. He's 28
years old, with a black leather cap, a denim vest and a black
T-shirt. He's clean shaven with short brown hair and a slight
build.

Rebecca lands a tough shot, then pumps her fist and yelps. Bill
turns to look. He studies her a few moments, then turns back
to his empty glass. He starts crushing peanuts in the shell by
pounding his fist on the bar.

Rebecca looks at him and lets out a laugh. She shakes her head
and resumes her game. Bill turns to face her.

                         BILL
          What's so funny?

                       REBECCA
          You.

Rebecca takes a shot, two balls dropping in separate pockets.

                         BILL
          Me?

Rebecca shakes her head and looks away.

                         BILL
          What?

                       REBECCA
          Oh, you don't want to know.

                         BILL
          Try me.

                       REBECCA
          You think you're some kind of badass, don't
          you?

                         BILL
          Maybe I do.

Rebecca looks him up and down, then she goes back to studying
her next shot on the table.

                       REBECCA
          Sorry, but you have no idea what it means
          to be a badass.

                         BILL
          And I suppose you do?

                       REBECCA
                (to the bartender)
          Tell 'em, Jimbo.

JIMBO looks up from his newspaper. He's almost 60, almost bald,
big and burly, a bear in his own right.

                         JIMBO
          No thanks, I'm out of this one.

                         REBECCA
          Pussy.
               (to Bill)
          What are you lookin' at?

                         BILL
          That's what I'm trying to figure out.

Rebecca swigs the last of her beer, then puts the bottle on the
bar.

                         REBECCA
          Hit me again.

                         JIMBO
          I don't think so.

                         REBECCA
          Come on, gimme a break.

                         JIMBO
          No way. You're done.

                         REBECCA
          Bastard.

                         BILL
          You know, there's something about you. It's
          your eyes. You look familiar.

                         REBECCA
          Yeah. That's a good one. You should write
          that one down.

                         BILL
          No, I'm serious. What's your name?

                         REBECCA
               (sighs, looks away)
          Whatever.

>   BILL
> Nice to meet you, Miss Whatever.

>   REBECCA
>   (shaking her head)
> Oh brother. You're a jackass, you know
> that?

She throws a handful of peanuts at Bill's chest.

>   REBECCA
> Fuckhead.

>   JIMBO
> Look here, if you two want to start
> something, take it outside.

>   REBECCA
> Go fuck yourself.

>   JIMBO
> Yeah, fuck you too.

>   REBECCA
>   (to Bill)
> What are you smirking at?

>   BILL
> I like a woman with a dirty mouth.

>   REBECCA
> Oh yeah? I've got a few other parts of me
> that are just as dirty.

>   BILL
> Really?

>   REBECCA
> Yeah.

>   BILL
> That's very enticing.

>   REBECCA
> Enticing? What, do you go to college or
> something?

                         BILL
          Do I look like a college student?

                       REBECCA
          Then where do you get your fancy words
          from? Do you read poetry?

                         BILL
          I read books. Maybe you've heard of them.

Rebecca lifts the empty beer bottle from the bar. She holds it
by the neck, ready to swing.

                       REBECCA
          Look, if you want me to smash this in your
          face, just say so.

                        JIMBO
          Okay, that's it. Both of you. Outside. Now.

                       REBECCA
          What? I didn't even touch him.

                        JIMBO
          I can't afford any more of your shit. I
          don't need the police here again. Get out.
          Both of you. Now.

Jimbo shows a gun. Not menacingly. He's done this routine
before.

                       REBECCA
          Fine. I'm only leaving 'cause I've got
          better things to do. Asshole.

EXT. CIRCLE J BAR — DUSK

Bill follows Rebecca through the door. She looks up at the
darkening sky then kicks at the dirt with her shoe.

                       REBECCA
          Thanks a lot.

                         BILL
          There are other bars you can go to.

                    REBECCA
        Not any with Jimbo. He may be an asshole
        but he gives me free drinks.

                     BILL
        What? Why the hell does he do that?

                    REBECCA
        I don't know. I guess 'cause he's my dad.

                     BILL
        You called him a pussy.

                    REBECCA
        Yeah. So?

                     BILL
        Okay. Never mind.

The two stare at each other, waiting, daring the other to make
a move. Finally Rebecca pulls out a switchblade, stabs the
front tire of a motorcycle, then the back tire, then kicks it
over. It rocks back and forth on the ground for a few seconds.

                    REBECCA
        What do you think of that?

                     BILL
        Nice job. That's my bike.

                    REBECCA
        Really?

                     BILL
        Yeah.

Rebecca looks at the bike. She notices a small round mirror
lying loose on the ground. She picks it up and looks at
herself, adjusting her hair. The mirror is unbroken.

                    REBECCA
        You should have said something.

                     BILL
        Yeah, well . . .

                    REBECCA
          Sorry.

Rebecca hands the mirror to Bill. He takes it.

                    BILL
          Thanks.

                    REBECCA
          You don't seem very upset. Most guys would
          be really pissed off right about now.

                    BILL
          Yeah, well, I'm not most guys.

Bill slowly circles his bike, surveying the damage.

                    REBECCA
          So . . . you're not upset?

                    BILL
          I'm not happy about it. But what can I do?
          What's done is done. You know?

                    REBECCA
          Yeah. I guess.

                    BILL
          If you weren't so damned fast with a
          knife . . .

                    REBECCA
          Look, I said I was sorry. What more do you
          want?

                    BILL
          I want new tires for my bike.

Bill absently hands the mirror back to Rebecca. She takes it.

                    REBECCA
          Fine, I'll buy you two new tires. All
          right? Big crybaby.

                    BILL
          No, forget it. You don't have to.

                    REBECCA
Good. I can't afford to buy shit.

                    BILL
But you owe me a ride home. I live on the
other side of town.

                    REBECCA
You're gonna have to call a cab. I don't
have any wheels.

                    BILL
That's great. How do you get places?

                    REBECCA
I walk. Or I get a ride. I'm not rich.

                    BILL
We're all rich. In proportion to the things
we can afford to leave alone.

                    REBECCA
        (thinks a moment)
What the hell does that mean?

                    BILL
It means whatever you want it to mean.

Bill struggles to lift the motorcycle upright. He leans it
against the side of the building.

                    REBECCA
I think you're a phony.

                    BILL
If you say so.

Bill wipes his hands on his vest and stares at his bike.

                    REBECCA
You're no badass, I know that.

                    BILL
Yeah, maybe you're right. Or maybe you're
dead wrong.

                    REBECCA
Okay, tell me, what's the worst thing you
ever done?

                    BILL
Me?

                    REBECCA
Yeah, you, Mr. Badass.

                    BILL
I shot a man just to watch him die.

                    REBECCA
Yeah, that's bullshit. Don't fuck with me.

Rebecca shoves him by pushing on his arm. Bill moves in closer.

                    BILL
You have nice eyes.

                    REBECCA
You're some kind of pansyass choirboy,
aren't you?

                    BILL
I burned down a church once. Lit it on
fire.

                    REBECCA
For real?

                    BILL
There's a vacant lot on Penbrook. That used
to be a church. Fifteen years ago.

                    REBECCA
Why did you do that?

                    BILL
I don't know. I felt like it.

                    REBECCA
Shit.

                    BILL
What about you? What have you done?

                    REBECCA
Me? Where do I start? I got a rap sheet a
hundred times longer than your dick.

                    BILL
You haven't seen my dick.

                    REBECCA
I've seen plenty of dicks. I'm guessing
you're average. At best.

                    BILL
You like asking for trouble, don't you?

                    REBECCA
How many times have you been busted? Once?
Twice? Never?

                    BILL
That's no way to measure anything.

                    REBECCA
Why the hell not?

                    BILL
Because I'm not stupid enough to get
caught.

                    REBECCA
Are you callin' me stupid?

                    BILL
No. I'm saying there are two kinds of evil
in this world. Smart and not-so-smart. The
not-so-smart kind, they die off pretty
quick. Natural selection. The smart, they
become lawyers and generals and presidents.
CEOs.

                    REBECCA
What the fuck are you talkin' about?

                    BILL
I'm talking about murder, mass murder,
grand theft. It goes on every day. But no
one sees it, so no one says anything, and
no one gets busted. It just keeps going on
and on. Until the world is upside down. The
crazy people get to decide what's wrong and
what's right. Because they have the power.
That's all that counts in the end. Power.

                    REBECCA
You went to college, didn't you?

                    BILL
I dropped out.

                    REBECCA
How come?

                    BILL
I kept thinking about things. Way too much.

                    REBECCA
Yeah? Like what?

                    BILL
Like how I wanted to do stuff. Crazy stuff.
Something really big. And bad.

                    REBECCA
How bad?

                    BILL
Real bad. The kind that would make the
news. The kind that people would talk about
for years.

                    REBECCA
You're just bullshittin' me.

                    BILL
Why would I do that?

                    REBECCA
I don't know. I guess because you want to
fuck me.

                         BILL
          Is that a crime?

                       REBECCA
          No, that's not a crime. Lyin' to me about
          who you are, that's a crime.

                         BILL
          How could I lie to that pretty little face
          of yours?

                       REBECCA
          You're so full of shit.

                         BILL
          You're even prettier when you smile.

                       REBECCA
          Yeah. Fuck you.

                         BILL
          Such a little spitfire.

Rebecca spits on him. Bill laughs at first, then pins her
against the wall. She smiles and spits again. He smiles and
kisses her. People walk nearby. Bill takes notice and lets her
loose.

                         BILL
          Let's go somewhere.

                       REBECCA
          No.

                         BILL
          Why not?

                       REBECCA
          Meet me back here. Tomorrow night.
          Midnight. Do something bad, as bad as you
          can manage, and bring proof. I'll do the
          same. We'll compare notes and see who wins.

                         BILL
          A contest?

                         REBECCA
          You got it.

                           BILL
          And if I win?

                         REBECCA
          You get your wish. You get to fuck me.

                           BILL
          And if you win?

                         REBECCA
          I get to hurt you. For lyin' to me.

Bill looks her up and down. Then he smiles and nods.

                           BILL
          This could be fun.

Rebecca turns to leave.

                           BILL
          Wait. What are we talking about here?
          Vandalism, theft, arson, what?

                         REBECCA
          Whatever you want to do . . . do it. There
          are no rules. Except one. Don't get caught.

Bill smiles as he watches her walk away.

EXT. BILL'S HOUSE — NIGHT

Bill steps out of a taxi and pays the driver. He walks up to
his house. He pauses on the front steps to breathe in the night
air. Then he heads for the door.

INT. BILL'S HOUSE — NIGHT

Bill moves quietly through a darkened hall. He gets halfway up
the stairs before he stops cold at the sound of a voice.

                           MOM
          Billy, is that you?

                          BILL
          Yes.

                          MOM
          It's so late.

                          BILL
          I told you I'd be late.

                          MOM
          Be sure and lock up.
               (pause)
          Billy, did you hear me?

                          BILL
          Yes, Mom.

Bill enters his room. It's impeccably clean, modern, stylized
in white and black. He tosses his cap on a leather chair. For
several seconds he stands staring at a door on the opposite
wall.

Bill retrieves a hidden key from above the door frame. He
unlocks the door and opens it. He clicks the overhead light.
It's a walk-in closet, with chaos inside — books, equipment,
boxes, strange tools and supplies. Echoes of Picasso's
Guernica.

He picks up a tiny carved wooden box, turns off the light,
closes the door and locks it, all with an air of solemnity.

Bill sits down on the bed. He opens the box and pulls out a
match and strikes it against the side. He watches it burn down
to his fingers, at which point he snuffs it out with a quick
twist of his thumb. He holds perfectly still for a few seconds.

He looks at his singed skin. Then he closes his eyes to savor
the lingering pain, his face still devoid of any expression.

INT. REBECCA'S APARTMENT — NIGHT

Rebecca steps inside, closes and locks the door. The floor is
strewn with clothes and food wrappers. She takes off her shoes
and rubs the bottoms of her feet. She presses a button on her
blinking answering machine.

                    MACHINE VOICE
          You have one new message. Sent today at
          11:35 PM.

                    LENNY
          Hey, it's me. I thought you were coming
          over tonight. I waited. Anyway, I'm goin'
          to bed now. I had a long day.

The machine clicks, then starts blinking.

Rebecca sits on the bed and swigs a drink from a vodka bottle
on the nightstand. Then she turns off the light and curls up
in bed with a jumbo-sized Love-A-Lot Bear. She still has all of
her clothes on.

INT. KITCHEN — MORNING

MOM clanks dishes in the sink. She's 48 years old, with
blonde hair turned prematurely gray in most places. It's clear
that she was once a very attractive woman, but now she looks
unconcerned about her appearance. She wears an almost perpetual
frown.

Mom sits down at the table where Bill is reading from a folded
newspaper. She stares at him for a long moment but he does not
look up.

                    MOM
          I heard you come in. You were out awfully
          late last night.

                    BILL
          Yeah.

                    MOM
          Did you meet someone?

                    BILL
               (pause)
          Yeah.

                    MOM
          A girl?

                        BILL
A woman.

                        MOM
Well, that's nice. You can bring her around
sometime.

                        BILL
No. It's not like that.

                        MOM
What, I can't meet her?

                        BILL
Mom.

                        MOM
What is she? A prostitute?

                        BILL
Mom.

                        MOM
I should be able to meet who you're dating.

                        BILL
We're not dating. Not really.

                        MOM
Are you two having sex?

                        BILL
God, please.

                        MOM
You need to be careful. You know that,
don't you?

                        BILL
Yes, I know. I'm not stupid.

                        MOM
So what's her name?

Bill looks down at his newspaper.

                    MOM
          Come now. She must have a name.

                    BILL
          I don't know her name, all right? Stop it,
          don't look at me like that.

                    MOM
          What's wrong with Amy? If you ask her out,
          I'm sure she'd say yes. Should I call her
          for you?

                    BILL
          No. Don't do that. Please.

                    MOM
          She's a nice girl.

                    BILL
          Yes, she's very nice.

                    MOM
          Is that the problem? She's too nice? You
          need a nasty girl? Someone to spank your
          bottom?

Bill heaves a sigh and walks out.

INT. REBECCA'S APARTMENT — MORNING

Rebecca wakes up to her alarm clock. She turns it off and
throws it across the room. She takes a swig of vodka, then puts
the bottle back on the nightstand. She notices the motorcycle
mirror resting there.

Rebecca picks up the mirror and stares at herself. She frowns
and looks out the window. The morning sun is too bright and
she turns away. She puts down the mirror and picks up her cell
phone.

                    REBECCA
          Lydia? Can you cover for me today? I feel
          like shit. I can't come in.

                         LYDIA
          Honey, you're not on the schedule for
          today. This is Tuesday.

                         REBECCA
          Really? Are you sure?

                         LYDIA
          Yes, I'm sure. It's Tuesday. The day after
          Monday. You don't work today.

                         REBECCA
          Oh. Thank God. And you.

She hangs up and slides back into bed.

INT. BILL'S CAR — MORNING

Bill sits in his car, a plain white Buick. He thinks a moment
then picks up his cell phone.

                         BILL
          Hi. This is Bill. I can't come in today. My
          mom's really sick and I need to help her
          out. I should be in tomorrow. I hope.

                         VOICE
          Sure, Bill. That's no problem. We can
          manage.

                         BILL
          Great. Thanks.

Bill starts his car and drives. He gets on the highway and
drives a long way, to another town.

Eventually Bill finds himself sitting in his car outside a
bank. He pulls out a small notebook from the glove compartment
and writes in block letters: "I have a gun. Put money in the
bag." He thinks a moment, then writes another word: "Please."

He puts on dark sunglasses and his plain black cap. He picks up
an empty canvas satchel from the seat next to him.

He gets out of the car and stands staring at the bank.

EXT. CIRCLE J BAR — NIGHT

Rebecca sits on a tree stump. She's texting on her cell phone.
Bill walks up slowly. Rebecca doesn't see him at first.

                    BILL
          Hey.

                    REBECCA
          I didn't think you'd show up.

                    BILL
          I thought the same thing about you.

                    REBECCA
          Yeah, well, I'm here.

                    BILL
          Yeah. You are.

Rebecca stands and smiles faintly.

                    REBECCA
          So. What big crime did you do?

                    BILL
               (shrugs)
          Bank job.

                    REBECCA
          No way. Are you serious? You robbed a bank?

                    BILL
          Yeah.

                    REBECCA
          You're bullshittin' me.

                    BILL
          No. I'm serious.

                    REBECCA
          All right, which bank?

                    BILL
First Federal.

                  REBECCA
Where the hell is that?

                    BILL
Jackson.

                  REBECCA
Jackson? That's like 80 miles away.

                    BILL
Yep. I drove there and back.

                  REBECCA
What the hell for? There are banks right
here in town.

                    BILL
The police are smart. They know people
commit crimes within a comfort zone of 60
miles from their home. So if you want to
get away with a crime, you do it outside
that zone. If they don't catch you right
away, they're not gonna catch you. It's as
simple as that.

                  REBECCA
All right. How did you do it? Tell me.
Exactly.

                    BILL
I went in and asked for money.

                  REBECCA
Bullshit.

                    BILL
I handed the teller a note. It said I had
a gun. Tellers are trained to give money
if someone says they have a gun. It's the
magic word. Gun.

                  REBECCA
You really did it? A bank?

                    BILL
Yes.

                    REBECCA
Armed robbery?

                    BILL
Technically no. I didn't really have a gun.
But they didn't know that.

                    REBECCA
Christ, you really robbed a bank?

                    BILL
Yes, I told you.

                    REBECCA
         (looks him up and down)
I'm impressed.

                    BILL
So . . . what did you do?

                    REBECCA
I didn't do anything.

                    BILL
What do you mean?

                    REBECCA
I mean, I did nothing. Nothing at all.

                    BILL
Nothing? Why?

                    REBECCA
         (shrugs)
I wanted you to win.

                    BILL
Oh.
         (smiles, then suddenly frowns)
Shit.

                    REBECCA
What's the matter?

                              BILL
          I could've gotten myself a goddamned
          parking ticket. Right here in town. I
          didn't have to drive to Jackson and knock
          over a bank.

                            REBECCA
          Yeah, well, that's just a bonus.

                              BILL
          Fuck.

                            REBECCA
          Yeah. Go ahead.

Bill moves closer to Rebecca. He kisses her. Hard. She wraps
her arms around his neck. They really start to go at each
other, arms entwined, hands grasping all over. Then Rebecca
stops and pushes him back.

                            REBECCA
          Wait.

                              BILL
          What's wrong?

                            REBECCA
          How much money did you get?

                              BILL
          Why?

                            REBECCA
          Answer the question. How much?

                              BILL
          Forty-five hundred.

                            REBECCA
          Nice. That's a good day's work.

                              BILL
          Yeah.

                            REBECCA
          Show me.

                        BILL
        What?

                        REBECCA
        I want to see it.

                        BILL
        Sorry, I don't have it on me. But you're
        welcome to search me.

Bill raises his arms out to the sides.

                        REBECCA
        Take me to see it. Right now. I want to see
        the money.

                        BILL
        Why?

                        REBECCA
        Why? I want to make sure you're not lyin'
        to me. All you have to do is show me the
        damn money. And then I'll show you a damn
        good time.

                        BILL
        All right. Tomorrow.

                        REBECCA
        Why tomorrow? Why not now?

                        BILL
        I have it stashed.

                        REBECCA
        Stashed? You were supposed to bring proof.
        I told you.

                        BILL
        Tomorrow, okay? If that's not good
        enough . . .

                        REBECCA
        Fine, tomorrow. If you want to wait that
        long . . .

Rebecca puts one hand on her hip and strikes a sexy pose.

> BILL
>
> You're good.

> REBECCA
>
> Oh, you have no idea.

> BILL
>
> Tomorrow.

Bill points at her. Rebecca sighs, turns and walks away.

INT. RESTAURANT — MORNING

Rebecca and her waitress friend LYDIA are sitting in a booth counting tips after the breakfast crowd has left. Lydia is 55 years old, African American, with a pudgy face and sorrowful eyes.

> LYDIA
>
> Damn, you look tired.

> REBECCA
>
> I'm thinking I should get out of this town.
> For good.

> LYDIA
>
> Stop saying that. I need you to stick
> around. You're the only sane person I know.

> REBECCA
>
> Shit, you're more pathetic than I am.

> LYDIA
>
> My daddy always told me, you might think
> your life is pretty bad, but there's always
> somebody worse off than you.

> REBECCA
>
> I'll drink to that.

Rebecca takes a sip from her Bloody Mary. She adds more vodka from a metal flask.

                    LYDIA
        You'll drink to anything.

                    REBECCA
        You should try this. It's delicious.

                    LYDIA
        No thanks. I don't drink before noon.

                    REBECCA
        How do you survive?

EXT. BILL'S HOUSE — LATE AFTERNOON

After work, Bill is walking from his car to his house. He sees
a kid running over his lawn, trampling his mom's flowers,
shooting an orange squirt gun at imaginary enemies.

                    BILL
        You shouldn't play with guns.

                    KID
        Why not?

                    BILL
        Someone could get killed.

                    KID
        It's only a squirt gun.

Bill steps closer to the boy and points his finger at him.

                    BILL
        Today it's a squirt gun, tomorrow it's
        a semi-automatic Glock pointed at your
        face. POW! Just like that, your fucking
        brains are blown out, all over the goddamn
        sidewalk.

The kid looks like he's going to cry. He turns and runs away.

                    BILL
        That's right. Run!

INT. BILL'S HOUSE — LATE AFTERNOON

Bill finds his mom working in the kitchen.

> BILL
> I'm just letting you know, I might be late
> tonight.

> MOM
> Again?

> BILL
> Yeah.

> MOM
> You need to get more sleep.

> BILL
> No, I need to get a life.

> MOM
> But dear . . .

> BILL
> Look, if you want me to move out, I will.

> MOM
> No, I'm not saying that.

> BILL
> I need to make my own decisions.

> MOM
> Of course, I would never try to tell you
> what to do. Or how to live.

> BILL
> Good.

Bill starts to leave, thinking the matter is settled.

> MOM
> I just want you to be careful.

Bill sighs.

                              MOM
               And not do anything stupid.

Bill throws up his arms in despair. He turns and walks out of
the house.

EXT. CIRCLE J BAR — NIGHT

Bill pulls up in his car. Rebecca is waiting for him in the
same spot. Bill turns off the engine but does not get out of
the car.

                              BILL
               Get in.

                            REBECCA
               What? Where are we going?

                              BILL
               Just get in, I'll show you.

Rebecca hesitates.

                              BILL
               Come on. Don't look so worried.

                            REBECCA
               I'm not afraid of you. I've got a knife and
               I know how to use it.

                              BILL
               Yeah, I know. Get in.

Rebecca gets in the car.

                            REBECCA
               What kind of car is this anyway? Is this a
               Buick?

                              BILL
               I need a respectable car for work. I prefer
               my Harley but I still need to get new tires
               for it, thank you very much.

>   REBECCA
>   Yeah, well, get over it.

>   BILL
>   Put your seatbelt on.

>   REBECCA
>   What? You're kidding, right?

>   BILL
>   No, I'm not. Put it on.

Rebecca offers a heavy sigh but obeys. Bill starts the car and
drives.

>   REBECCA
>   Jesus, this feels so wrong. A Buick. It
>   must be perfect for robbing banks. It's so
>   boring it's almost invisible.

>   BILL
>   Yeah.

Bill drives to the front of a classy hotel, the best in town. A
valet approaches.

>   REBECCA
>   What the hell? Is this for real?

>   BILL
>   If we're going to do this, we might as well
>   do it right.

Bill flashes a hotel key.

INT. HOTEL LOBBY — NIGHT

Bill leads Rebecca by the hand through the lobby. Rebecca
stares at everything. She's never been here before.

INT. HOTEL ROOM — NIGHT

Bill opens the door and lets Rebecca walk in first. She looks
around and puts her hands on her hips.

                    REBECCA
Okay, where is it?

                    BILL
You don't want to relax? Sit down, have
a drink, enjoy the view? There's a fully
stocked minibar and a great view of the
town. Quite romantical, as they say.

                    REBECCA
Fuck that. Where's the goddamned money?

                    BILL
You're very impatient. You know that?

                    REBECCA
The money. Or I'm outta here.

                    BILL
The bag on the table.

Rebecca moves quickly. She lifts the canvas bag and turns it
over. A stream of loose bills falls out.

                    REBECCA
Damn. You weren't kidding. This is
beautiful. Is this forty-five hundred?

                    BILL
Yeah. You're welcome to count it.

                    REBECCA
This is really nice. I could get used to
this. What's my cut?

                    BILL
Your cut?

                    REBECCA
Yeah.

                    BILL
Why should I give you a cut?

                              REBECCA
          Why? I inspired you. You wouldn't have
          robbed a bank without me.

                                BILL
          I guess.

                              REBECCA
          Oh, come on. You did it because you want
          to get into my pants. You want to fuck me.
          Admit it.

                                BILL
          Okay, yeah, I do. But we have a problem
          here.

                              REBECCA
          What?

                                BILL
          If I give you money, that would make you a
          prostitute. Wouldn't it?

                              REBECCA
          What's your point?

                                BILL
          You don't have a problem with that?

                              REBECCA
          Everyone's a prostitute. Everyone takes
          the money. The only difference is how much
          money they get.

                                BILL
          Well, fine, if it's money you want . . .
          you can have it.

                              REBECCA
          For real? How much?

                                BILL
          All of it.

                    REBECCA
          Are you kidding? You mean it?

                    BILL
          Yeah, I mean it.

Bill moves closer to Rebecca. He has a determined look in his
eyes. Rebecca notices and starts to back away. Bill grabs her
and pins her arms against a wall. Their faces are inches apart.

                    BILL
          You just have to tell me one thing first.

                    REBECCA
          What?

                    BILL
          You have to say "I'm a cheap fucking
          whore." Say it.

                    REBECCA
          I'm a cheap . . . fucking . . . whore.

They really go at it this time. Loud and wild. Grunting and grabbing.
Knocking over a chair and a lamp. It's so wild it's almost comical.

LATER

Half-dressed, Rebecca sits at the side of the bed, playing with
money on the nightstand. Bill is staring up at the ceiling with
a peaceful smile on his face.

                    REBECCA
          I like this. This is really nice.

                    BILL
          Yeah. That's what I was thinking.

                    REBECCA
          We need to do it again.

                    BILL
          Definitely.
              (pause)
          Wait, what are we talking about?

                    REBECCA
          (waving a handful of money)
This.

                    BILL
Oh.

                    REBECCA
Think of all the banks outside our comfort
zone.

                    BILL
Wait a minute.

                    REBECCA
We could make a killing.

                    BILL
Or get killed.

                    REBECCA
Forty-five hundred dollars. Do you know how
long it takes me to make that much?

                    BILL
Maybe you need a better job. What do you
do anyway? When you're not sleeping with
assholes like me?

                    REBECCA
What I do is none of your business.

                    BILL
Okay.

Rebecca turns away from him. She keeps staring at the money.

                    BILL
Can you at least tell me your name? Now
that we've . . .

                    REBECCA
No.

                    BILL
        Can I tell you mine?

                    REBECCA
        No.

                    BILL
        You're not making this easy.

                    REBECCA
        Shut up. I'm trying to think.

Bill shuts up for a while. He stares at the ceiling. He's
frowning now.

                    BILL
        I don't want to make a living robbing
        banks.

                    REBECCA
        Fine. I don't need your help.

                    BILL
        Look, I don't know what's going on in that
        head of yours, but it's not smart to . . .

                    REBECCA
        Don't tell me what's smart. Okay? I'm not
        some kind of idiot.

                    BILL
        No, I'm only saying . . .

                    REBECCA
        Just shut up. Okay?

                    BILL
        But . . .

                    REBECCA
        I think you should go.

                    BILL
        Oh, come on . . .

                         REBECCA
              Just go. Get out. Now.   .

Bill puts on his clothes. He picks up the room key and drops
it on the table next to the money. Bill watches her. She keeps
staring at the money. Bill leaves.

INT. BILL'S CAR — NIGHT

Bill sits in his car, staring at the steering wheel, trying
to decide what to do. He looks lost, alone. He finally shakes
himself from his trance and starts up his car.

EXT. BILL'S HOUSE — NIGHT

Bill parks his car in the driveway and walks up to his house.
On the way, he finds an orange squirt gun. He picks it up, then
sits on the porch with the gun in his hands. He stares at the
gun, then closes his eyes, leans his head back and waits for
the dawn.

INT. LENNY'S APARTMENT — DAY

LENNY sits on the couch with a beer bottle in one hand and a
remote control in the other. He's watching an old football game
on the classic sports channel. He's wearing a stained white
muscle shirt. He's 30 years old, handsome in a ragged way.

Rebecca walks in, not bothering to knock. She has her own key.
She's carrying a bag.

                         REBECCA
              Hey, asshole. Turn that thing off.

Lenny mutes the sound and checks his watch.

                         LENNY
              What took you so long? You said three
              thirty.

                         REBECCA
              I bought you some presents.

> LENNY

Yeah? What the hell for? It's not my
birthday.

> REBECCA

I know. I just wanted to do something nice.
It's not a crime.

> LENNY

Depends on what you bought. What is all
this shit?

> REBECCA

Open them up and find out.

Lenny doesn't move. Rebecca picks a gift and hands it to him.
He peels off the wrapping to reveal a small plush gorilla. He
turns it over, trying to find some explanation.

> REBECCA

It reminded me of you. It's cute.
>   (pause)
You don't like it.

> LENNY

What else you got?

> REBECCA

Here.

Rebecca hands him another gift. He opens it. In an elaborate
silver frame, a snapshot of Rebecca rests at a slight angle.
It's too small for the frame.

> LENNY

A picture?

> REBECCA

Yeah. You know, so you can see me when I'm
not around.

> LENNY

Okay.

Lenny stares at it a while. He's not sure what to do with it.
Finally he puts it down on the couch.

> REBECCA
> Here. Open this one. I know you'll like it.

Rebecca hands him a box. It's not wrapped. Lenny opens it and
his face lights up. It's a 9mm Glock.

> LENNY
> Hey, cool. A gun.

> REBECCA
> Not just any gun. The one you said you
> wanted. Remember?

> LENNY
> Are there bullets?

> REBECCA
> Bullets?

> LENNY
> Yeah, a gun's no good without ammo. Where'd
> you get the money for this stuff? You're
> always complaining about how broke you are.

> REBECCA
> Yeah, well, when I'm not with you, I turn
> tricks.

> LENNY
> Right. How about the truth?

> REBECCA
> The truth? Bank robbery.

> LENNY
> Okay, forget it.

> REBECCA
> That's better.

Lenny keeps playing with the gun. Rebecca watches him, waiting
for a thank you that never comes.

INT. BILL'S OFFICE — DAY

Bill is sitting at his desk, staring at nothing. He turns in
his chair to stare out the window. He picks up a small stack of
papers, then puts it back down and stares out the window again.

EXT. USED CAR LOT — DAY

Rebecca is wearing her waitress uniform, walking past a row of
used cars. She stops and turns to eye a conservative red sedan,
a Buick. It's 15 years old, but the price is right: 2,995.

INT. GUN SHOP — DAY

Bill looks at a case of guns. He points to a silver revolver.
The clerk takes it from the case and hands it to Bill. It's
the first time he has ever held a gun. He looks worried, almost
terrified.

A few feet away from Bill, Lenny stands with his hands resting
on two boxes of bullets.

EXT. RESTAURANT — DAY

Rebecca pulls up in her new car. She drags Lydia out of the
restaurant to show it off. Lydia is impressed. The two laugh
and hug.

EXT. CIRCLE J BAR — NIGHT

Bill pulls up in the parking lot, two spaces away from
Rebecca's new car.

INT. CIRCLE J BAR — NIGHT

Bill walks in and sees Rebecca. She's wearing a Circle J
baseball cap. Bill approaches her, but she walks away. He
follows.

                    BILL
          Hey.

                    REBECCA
          What do you want?

                    BILL
        I want to talk.

                    REBECCA
        Go fuck yourself.

                    BILL
        No thanks. It's more fun with you.

Rebecca just stares at him. She's not amused.

                    BILL
        I came here to show you something.

                    REBECCA
            What?

Bill turns to look at the bartender, Jimbo, who is eyeing Bill
with suspicion.

                    BILL
        Not here. Outside.

                    REBECCA
        Yeah, go to hell.

                    BILL
        Aren't you the least bit curious?

                    REBECCA
            (sighs)
        This better be good.

EXT. CIRCLE J BAR — NIGHT

Bill and Rebecca exit the bar and walk past Rebecca's car. She
does not point it out to Bill. The two walk behind the bar.
Bill opens his denim jacket and produces his new gun.

                    BILL
        Look at that.

                    REBECCA
        So?

                    BILL
You're not impressed?

                  REBECCA
Should I be?

                    BILL
I bought a gun.

                  REBECCA
You <u>bought</u> it? Wow, you're such a badass.
Did you say "please" and "thank you"?

                    BILL
What?

                  REBECCA
If you're a real badass, you don't buy a
gun. You steal it. Or you pry it from the
hands of a dead body. You don't go to a
store and <u>buy</u> one.

                    BILL
A gun is a gun. It doesn't matter how I got
it, this thing can still fuck someone up.
For real.

Bill toys with the gun, pointing it toward the sky.

                  REBECCA
Is that some kind of threat?

                    BILL
You sound like you want me to use this
thing. On <u>you</u>.

Rebecca puts one hand on her hip.

                  REBECCA
Maybe I do. Or maybe you don't have the
balls.

                    BILL
You don't want to live, do you?

> REBECCA
> Let's face it, by the time this thing is
> over, one of us is going to be dead. If
> we're lucky, maybe both of us.

> BILL
> So what you're saying is . . . you're
> totally messed up.

> REBECCA
> What I'm saying is you've got to be willing
> to give up everything. There's no tomorrow,
> there's only right now. You suffer pain or
> you cause it. You kill or you die. You fuck
> or you fuck off.

> BILL
> Win or lose? All or nothing?

> REBECCA
> You got it. What's it gonna be?

Rebecca moves closer to Bill, with both hands on her hips now.

> BILL
> You're crazy.

> REBECCA
> I know. I win.

> BILL
> No. Not yet.

Rebecca grabs Bill's shirt and pulls him close, close enough to
kiss, but she stops herself.

> REBECCA
> Let's do something.

> BILL
> What do you have in mind?

> REBECCA
> Something wild. Something fun.

She flashes a mischievous smile.

EXT. BILL'S CAR — NIGHT

Rebecca is hanging out Bill's car window with a baseball bat in her hands. Bill casts nervous glances at her as he drives along a darkened rural road.

> BILL
> Um, I don't think this is such a good idea.

> REBECCA
> Hell, this is great. Drive faster.

> BILL
> No.

> REBECCA
> Come on. Don't be a pussy.

Bill drives faster. Three mailboxes get whacked. The last one slams into the car causing damage to the front panel.

A big REDNECK GUY just arriving home sees his mailbox get destroyed. He jumps in his car and pursues Bill's Buick. A long and wild chase ensues. Bill and Rebecca manage to escape when their pursuer spins out on a turn and slides off the road.

> BILL
> Okay. Let's not do that again.

> REBECCA
> What do you mean? That was fun.

> BILL
> This isn't my idea of fun.

> REBECCA
> Why not?

> BILL
> I don't like being chased all over town.

> REBECCA
> Fine. What's your idea of fun?

                    BILL
I like to plan things. I don't like
surprises. Too many things can go wrong.
I'm not a big fan of accidental death and
dismemberment.

                    REBECCA
All right. Let's plan something. Something
big.

                    BILL
Like what?

                    REBECCA
A bank job.

                    BILL
No.

                    REBECCA
Yes.

                    BILL
No.

INT. BANK — DAY

Canned music drones through the air. Bill and Rebecca stand
awkwardly next to each other near the lobby door.

                    BILL
No. We can't.

                    REBECCA
Be quiet.

                    BILL
We can't do this. Not like this.

                    REBECCA
Shut up. We drove 80 miles. We're here.
We're doing it.

                    BILL
No.

                         REBECCA
          Yes.

                          BILL
          No. It doesn't feel right.

                         REBECCA
          I don't give a shit what you feel. Okay?

                          BILL
          Fuck you.

                         REBECCA
          No, fuck you!

Rebecca slaps Bill's chest. A bald pot-bellied MANAGER
approaches.

                         MANAGER
          Look, if you two want to go at it, that's
          fine. But you need to do it somewhere else.

                         REBECCA
          Hear that? He wants us to do it.

                         MANAGER
          No. That's not what I meant.

                         REBECCA
          And I bet you want to watch. Am I right,
          fat boy?

                          BILL
          Please, shut up.

                         REBECCA
          No, you shut up. Asshole.

Bill picks her up and carries her out the door. She's kicking
her legs, punching his back and screaming.

EXT. PARKING LOT — DAY

Bill walks with Rebecca hoisted on his shoulder. He puts her
down near his car.

                         REBECCA
          What the fuck did you do that for?

                           BILL
          Oh, I don't know, because you were losing
          your mind?

                         REBECCA
          Damn it, we could have been rich by now.

                           BILL
          Or arrested. Or shot.

                         REBECCA
          You had to be a chicken shit. You couldn't
          be a man for two goddamned minutes, could
          you?

                           BILL
          Lay off, all right?

                         REBECCA
          Take me home.

                           BILL
          What?

                         REBECCA
          I don't want to do this anymore. I want to
          go home.

Bill sighs and shakes his head.

                         REBECCA
          I mean it, I'm through with this shit.

                           BILL
          Fine.

Bill slowly approaches his car. Rebecca spies a vintage
convertible parked halfway down the street. She runs toward it.
Bill follows at a brisk walk. The top is down and Rebecca jumps
in the driver's side without opening the door.

                         REBECCA
          Get in.

                          BILL
          This doesn't belong to you.

                         REBECCA
          No shit. Get in.

Bill opens the door and gets in. Rebecca goes at him, kissing
him wildly. She takes off her shirt, showing a lacy red bra.

                          BILL
          What are you doing?

                         REBECCA
          You.

                          BILL
          We can't do it here.

                         REBECCA
          All right.

She pulls out her switchblade and starts hotwiring the car.
Bill is fascinated watching her.

                          BILL
          No, don't do that. Stop.

EXT. COUNTRY ROAD — DAY

Rebecca and Bill are speeding along in the stolen convertible.
Rebecca is driving. She lets her hair loose. She's smiling,
beaming. She's not wearing her shirt. Bill looks happy too.

EXT. COUNTRY FIELD — DAY

Tall grasses and trees surround the ruins of a barn and silo.
Rebecca and Bill are lying on a blanket next to the stolen car.
She's holding a handful of daisies, plucking petals off one by
one. She's still not wearing her shirt.

                          BILL
          Do you believe in God?

                    REBECCA
          Sometimes. Maybe.

                    BILL
          That's not an answer.

                    REBECCA
          Yes it is.

                    BILL
          No it's not.

                    REBECCA
          Sometimes I feel like the world is
          pointless and stupid. And sometimes I feel
          like it makes perfect sense.

                    BILL
          What about right now? What do you feel
          right now?

                    REBECCA
          Right now . . . I feel good. Like anything
          is possible. Like I could change the world.
          If I wanted to.

                    BILL
          I believe you could.

Rebecca turns slowly to Bill and grins.

                    REBECCA
          You got any candy?

                    BILL
          Actually, I do.

Bill produces a small box of Red Hots from his pocket. Rebecca
just shakes her head.

                    REBECCA
          That's not what I meant.

                    BILL
          You said candy.

                    REBECCA
          Not that kind.

                    BILL
          It's all I have.

                    REBECCA
          Never mind. Forget it.
               (sighs)
          You are such a goddamned choirboy. Got any
          cigarettes?

                    BILL
          I don't smoke.

                    REBECCA
          Then why do you carry matches? I saw you.
          At the bar.

                    BILL
          Yeah. You never know when you're going to
          need to light something on fire.

                    REBECCA
          Like a church?

Bill looks at her and smiles. He's pleased she remembers, and
believes him.

                    REBECCA
          Didn't your mommy ever teach you about
          playing with matches?

                    BILL
          Didn't your dad ever teach you about
          meeting strange men in bars?

                    REBECCA
          You're not that strange.

                    BILL
          You don't know me very well.

Rebecca casts him a curious and cynical look, trying to figure
him out.

                    BILL
I have an idea.

Bill stands up and extends his hand down to Rebecca. She just
stares at him.

                    BILL
The trees can be witnesses.

                  REBECCA
For what?

Rebecca reaches up and takes his hand. The two stand facing
each other. Bill holds both of her hands.

                    BILL
I . . . take you . . . whatever your name
is . . . to be my unlawfully wedded wife.
To have and to hold, for richer or poorer,
in sickness and in health, forsaking all
others, from this day forward, for as long
as we both shall live.
      (pauses to admire her)
If anyone knows just cause why these two
should not be joined together, let him
speak now or forever keep quiet about it.

Rebecca looks around at the trees. Then she looks at Bill and
tilts her head, waiting.

                    BILL
Now it's your turn. Do you take me?

                  REBECCA
      (smirking)
Maybe.

                    BILL
Come on. Take me.

                  REBECCA
Well . . .

                    BILL
Oh come on.

                    REBECCA
          I promise . . . to put up with you for a
          while . . . take you for granted . . . and
          eventually hate you so much I want to kill
          you in your sleep. How's that?

                    BILL
          Good enough. I now pronounce us husband and
          wife. You may now . . .

Rebecca jumps on him. They fall back on the grass in a tangle
of limbs. They start kissing and groping in a passionate
frenzy.

                    REBECCA
          Hey, wait a minute. Do I get a ring?

                    BILL
          What?

                    REBECCA
          A ring. We're married now, right?

                    BILL
          Yeah, okay. I'll get you one.

                    REBECCA
          Really? You mean it? A real one?

                    BILL
          Yeah.

                    REBECCA
          Cool.

                    BILL
          But you can't hock it. You have to keep it.
          And wear it.

                    REBECCA
          Yeah, we'll see.

Rebecca flings off her bra and throws her body against Bill.

LATER

Rebecca wakes up in Bill's arms. She blinks a few times, then looks up into his eyes.

>   REBECCA
>   You know how to make a bomb?

>   BILL
>   What?

>   REBECCA
>   I want to blow something up. Something big.

>   BILL
>   That's terrorism.

>   REBECCA
>   No. It's vandalism. Just big. I want to do
>   something big. I want to change something.
>   I want to leave a mark. Like I was here.
>   You know what I mean. Don't you?

>   BILL
>   Yeah. I do.

Rebecca gets up, goes to the car and starts searching through Bill's jacket.

>   REBECCA
>   Where's your gun?

>   BILL
>   I left it at home.

>   REBECCA
>   Damn it. You bastard.

Rebecca puts on Bill's jacket. The air is chilly now.

>   BILL
>   Yeah, as a matter of fact, I am a bastard.
>   My mom never married my dad, so yeah,
>   you're right.

Rebecca sits down next to him on the grass.

                    REBECCA
          Is that why you're so fucked up?

                    BILL
          Nah, I've only got myself to blame for
          that.

                    REBECCA
          So why didn't they get married?

                    BILL
          Hell, I don't know. I never thought of
          asking my mom about it. My dad died before
          I was born. Car accident.

                    REBECCA
          That sucks.

                    BILL
          I've seen old pictures of him but that's
          about it. It's funny . . . I ended up with
          my dad's first name and my mom's last name.

                    REBECCA
          That's weird.

                    BILL
          Yeah. I'm a weird guy.

Bill contorts his face into an almost psychotic expression.
Rebecca watches but does not react.

                    REBECCA
          You don't want to know more? About your
          dad?

                    BILL
          I figure what I don't know can't hurt me.
          None of that shit matters. There's only
          right now. You know?

                    REBECCA
          Yeah.

Rebecca snuggles up closer to Bill.

>   REBECCA
>   Your gun. Bring it next time. Okay?

INT. BILL'S HOUSE — DAY

Bill sits huddled in a corner of the living room. He's sitting
on the floor, holding a small notebook and a pen. He writes a
few words, then stops to stare out at nothing.

His mom walks in carrying a large framed picture of a big-eyed
urchin on black velvet. She looks around at the walls trying
to find the right place for it. She sees Bill sitting in the
corner, but she's not surprised to find him there.

She leans the picture against a chair and looks out the window.

>   MOM
>   Are you ever going to get that thing fixed?
>   How many days has it been now?

>   BILL
>   I'll take care of it. It's not your
>   problem.

>   MOM
>   I don't think it's good to leave your car
>   like that. It doesn't look safe.

>   BILL
>   Yes, Mom, it's perfectly safe. It just
>   looks bad.

>   MOM
>   You really should do something.

>   BILL
>   I will.

>   MOM
>   Good. Don't wait.

>   BILL
>   You know, I think that one would look
>   perfect in the back hallway.

Mom leaves with the picture. Bill goes back to writing.

EXT. CIRCLE J BAR   AFTERNOON

Rebecca sits texting on a tree stump. Her car is visible
nearby. When she sees Bill's car pull into the parking lot, she
quickly puts her phone away.

                    REBECCA
          We have to stop meeting like this.

                    BILL
          Get in.

                    REBECCA
          Your car is pretty fucked up.

                    BILL
          Yeah, thanks. Get in.

                    REBECCA
          Why can't we hang out here?

                    BILL
          With your dad watching? No thanks. Get in.

Rebecca gets in the car. Bill starts driving.

                    REBECCA
          So where are we going?

                    BILL
          You'll see.

                    REBECCA
          To buy me a ring?

                    BILL
          A ring? Whatever do you mean?

                    REBECCA
          Don't be an asshole. You promised. Hey,
          one of these nights we could break in
          somewhere. We could steal a ring.

                    BILL
    No, I don't think so.

                    REBECCA
    You owe me. I'm not going to forget.

                    BILL
    Yeah. Now that we're married, I have a
    question for you.

                    REBECCA
    Shoot.

                    BILL   '
    What's your name?

Rebecca shakes her head and looks away.

                    REBECCA
    I told you, I don't want to do that.

                    BILL
    Come on. Just your first name?

                    REBECCA
    I don't have a name. And neither do you.
    Until I give you one.

                    BILL
    If you say so.

                    REBECCA
    I do.

                    BILL
    Okay. Tell me something else then. What do
    you do for a living?

                    REBECCA
    I'm a prostitute. Remember?

                    BILL
    No, you're not. No bullshit. Remember?

                    REBECCA
What do you do?

                    BILL
For work?

                    REBECCA
Yeah. For work.

                    BILL
        (hesitates)
I work in an office.

                    REBECCA
And what exactly do you do in that office?
Jack off all day?

                    BILL
No.

                    REBECCA
Then what?

                    BILL
You're not going to believe it.

                    REBECCA
Try me.

                    BILL
I decide when people are going to die.

                    REBECCA
What the fuck? Are you telling me you kill
people for a living?

                    BILL
No. Not quite.

                    REBECCA
Then what?

                    BILL
I work for an insurance company.

                         REBECCA
          Oh, come on. You sell insurance? That's
          real nice. Some badass you are.

                         BILL
          I don't <u>sell</u> insurance. I don't sell
          anything. I'm an actuary. I figure out when
          people are going to croak so the company
          doesn't lose money.

                         REBECCA
          They pay you for that?

                         BILL
          Yeah. The pay is good and it gives me time
          to think.

                         REBECCA
          About what? Me?

Bill smiles and looks at her but does not answer.

                         REBECCA
          You're all fucked up, aren't you? Just like
          your car.

Bill keeps driving. Soon he parks his car in front of a fancy
restaurant. Rebecca looks surprised.

                         REBECCA
          What the hell? We can't eat here.

                         BILL
          We can do anything we want.

                         REBECCA
          Not if they kick us out for how we're
          dressed. Look at me. I'm dressed like . . .
          this.

                         BILL
          No problem. I have a plan.

SHOPPING MONTAGE

Bill takes Rebecca on a quick shopping trip. She tries on
fancy dresses, high-priced shoes, nice jewelry. She looks half
shocked, half delighted.

Bill picks out a sport coat and tie for himself. Rebecca vetoes
his choices and picks out a more stylish combination.

INT. FANCY RESTAURANT — NIGHT

Bill and Rebecca stare at each other over lobster and
champagne.

>   REBECCA
>   This is nice. I feel like a princess.

>   BILL
>   You should. You are.

Rebecca beams like a little girl.

INT. HOTEL SUITE — NIGHT

Rebecca walks in first. Bill follows close behind.

>   REBECCA
>   Hey, this is bigger than last time, isn't
>   it?

>   BILL
>   Yep. It's the best in the house.

>   REBECCA
>   Not bad.

>   BILL
>   It's the honeymoon suite.

>   REBECCA
>   And I'm your innocent virginal bride?

>   BILL
>   Sure, why not?

>   REBECCA
>   I'll show you why not.

Rebecca grabs him by the crotch.

>   BILL
>   Hey, wait a minute. I got you something.

Bill produces a tiny box and hands it to her.

>   REBECCA
>   No way. Really?

>   BILL
>   Go on, open it.

>   REBECCA
>   When did you do this? You said you didn't
>   have it.

>   BILL
>   Yeah, well . . . I lied.

Rebecca opens the box. Her face lights up.

>   REBECCA
>   Holy fuck. Is this thing real?

>   BILL
>   Yeah, it's real.

>   REBECCA
>   I mean, real diamonds?

>   BILL
>   Yeah. One hundred percent real. But you
>   can't sell it. Remember? You have to wear
>   it. You promised.

>   REBECCA
>   Christ. How the hell did you pay for this?
>   Did you rob another bank?

                    BILL
        No, this is legit. Nothing criminal about
        it.

                    REBECCA
        Hey, it fits me. This is so cool. I'm a
        fucking princess!

Bill laughs at her.

                    REBECCA
        What? What's so funny?

                    BILL
        I can't get enough of you.

                    REBECCA
        I know. You are so totally fucked up.

                    BILL
            (smiling)
        In a good way.

                    REBECCA
        Oh, you got that right . . .

                    BILL
        Yeah?

                    REBECCA
        Oh yeah . . . 'cause you ain't seen <u>nothin'</u>
        yet.

Rebecca throws herself at him with an especially wild fury.

EXT. AUTO BODY SHOP — MORNING

Bill drives up in his car. He gets out and hands the keys to
a skinny 20-year-old GREASE MONKEY. Lenny sits working in the
glass-walled office, but he and Bill do not meet. Bill starts
walking home.

INT. BILL'S HOUSE — DAY

Bill's mom is rearranging furniture in an unused upstairs
bedroom. She spills a shoebox of old photos onto the floor. She
picks up one of the photos. It shows Bill as a five-year-old
holding her hand. She smiles and props the photo on the table.

Kneeling down to scoop the rest of the photos back into the
box, she pauses at finding another snapshot. She stares at this
one for several seconds, her hand faintly shaking. She shuts
her eyes tightly.

INT. REBECCA'S APARTMENT — DUSK

Rebecca wakes to the sound of a phone ringing. She rolls over
but makes no effort to get out of bed. Her machine picks up.

                    LENNY
          Hey. You there? Pick up the phone. What,
          are you dead? Pick up the phone. Or turn on
          your cell. God damn it.

The machine clicks, then starts blinking.

Rebecca reaches to her nightstand and picks up the small round
mirror, her souvenir from Bill's bike. She tries adjusting her
hair and frowns at the result. She puts the mirror back and
looks at the ring on her hand. She smiles.

Rebecca gets out of bed and makes her way to the kitchen in
her underwear. She empties out her vodka bottle into the sink.
She pauses a moment, then downs the last few drops left in the
bottom.

INT. COFFEE SHOP — MORNING

Bill pays for a latte at a trendy upscale coffee shop. He stops
to look at a newspaper lying on a counter by the window. He
hears a truck sound its horn as it goes by and he looks up.

The truck passes to reveal Rebecca getting out of her red Buick
in her waitress uniform. Bill watches her walk into the diner.

Bill walks quickly out of the shop, leaving his coffee behind.

INT. DINER — MORNING

Bill takes a seat in a booth. He keeps peering at Rebecca from
behind a tall menu.

                    LYDIA
          Good morning. May I take your order?

                    BILL
               (looking at Rebecca)
          I'm sorry, could I have another waitress?

                    LYDIA
          What? Because I'm black?

                    BILL
               (winces)
          No. God no. The blonde. I want her. I mean,
          I know her.

Lydia looks over at her friend, then looks back at Bill, sizing
him up.

                    LYDIA
          Move two tables down. She'll help you.

Bill moves to the other table. He keeps hiding behind the menu.
Rebecca approaches.

                    REBECCA
          Hi, welcome to Flannery's. Can I take your
          order?

                    BILL
               (lowering the menu)
          Hi.

                    REBECCA
          Jesus. What the fuck are you doing here?

                    BILL
          I'm hungry. I want something to eat.

                    REBECCA
               (sighs)
          Fine. What do you want?

Bill looks at the menu, then at Rebecca.

>   BILL
>   You.

>   REBECCA
>   You did <u>not</u> just say that.

>   BILL
>   (trying to be charming)   .
>   I think I did.

>   REBECCA
>   You have to order something that's on the
>   menu.

>   BILL
>   Well, actually I'm not really hungry.

>   REBECCA
>   I don't care. Order something.

>   BILL
>   Toast. With butter. How's the coffee here?

>   REBECCA
>   It's brown.

>   BILL
>   Okay . . .

>   REBECCA
>   Like shit.

>   BILL
>   In that case . . . I think I'll have orange
>   juice.

>   REBECCA
>   Is that it?

>   BILL
>   Yeah. So you're a waitress?

                    REBECCA
          No, this is just my day job. I'm actually a
          pole dancer.

                    BILL
          Really?

                    REBECCA
          No.

                    BILL
          Oh.

Rebecca heaves another sigh and walks away.

                    BILL
          Rebecca.

                    REBECCA
          What? What did you say?

                    BILL
          Nothing.

                    REBECCA
          My name . . . you said my name.

                    BILL
          No.

                    REBECCA
          How did you know my name?

                    BILL
          It's on your tag.

                    REBECCA
          God damn it.

Rebecca rips off the tag and flings it to the floor. Then she
storms out of the restaurant.

EXT. RESTAURANT PARKING LOT — DAY

Bill catches up with Rebecca outside. He grabs her elbow to
stop her.

>   BILL
>   Hey, I'm sorry. I wasn't trying . . .

>   REBECCA
>   Yeah, whatever.

>   BILL
>   Come on, really, it's no big deal.

>   REBECCA
>   I just like to keep things simple. You
>   know?

>   BILL
>   Yeah, well, I think we're past that point.

Bill stares at her for a long moment. Rebecca keeps looking
away, squinting into the wind.

>   BILL
>   Rebecca . . .

>   REBECCA
>   Please. Do not use my name. I hate hearing
>   it.

>   BILL
>   Why?

>   REBECCA
>   I told you. Names don't matter.

>   BILL
>   By any other name, you would smell as
>   sweet.

>   REBECCA
>   Yeah, right.
>   (faintly grinning)
>   I love it when you talk dirty.

                    BILL
I really like your name. I like the sound
of it. Do people ever call you Becky? Or
Becca?

                    REBECCA
No. Not if they want to live.

                    BILL
Hi. My name is Bill. Nice to meet you.

He smiles and extends his hand. She takes it.

                    REBECCA
Bill? William? Like a prince?

                    BILL
Yeah. Or a frog.

                    REBECCA
So what's your last name? Shakespeare?

                    BILL
No. My last name is Fartknocker. And since
you married me, you're Mrs. Fartknocker.

                    REBECCA
You're an idiot.

                    BILL
Well then, you married an idiot.

                    REBECCA
Yeah, I guess I did.

                    BILL
That's a nice car you got there. A Buick?

                    REBECCA
What?

                    BILL
I saw you driving it. You told me you
didn't have a car.

                         REBECCA
          Yeah, I just got it.

                           BILL
          Did you steal it?

                         REBECCA
          No, it's legit. One hundred percent.

                           BILL
          Where did you get the money?

                         REBECCA
          Where do you think? From you. That right
          there is your bank robbery.

                           BILL
          Really? Well, at least you put it to good
          use.

                         REBECCA
          Yeah, I'm not stupid.

                           BILL
          Hell, you're perfect.

Rebecca smirks and puts her hands on her hips.

                         REBECCA
          I like to think so.

                           BILL
          You better get back to work. So they don't
          fire that sweet little ass of yours.

Rebecca smiles and starts to walk back to the diner.

                           BILL
          Hey, when do you get off?

                         REBECCA
               (with a naughty smile)
          Whenever I feel like it.

                           BILL
          Get off <u>work</u>?

                    REBECCA
My shift ends at three.

                    BILL
Great. I'll meet you.

                    REBECCA
No. Let's do it Friday.

                    BILL
What? Why?

                    REBECCA
Because. If you keep spending every single
day and night with me, you'll get your own
sweet ass fired.

                    BILL
Yeah. So?

                    REBECCA
Then you might not be able to afford me.

                    BILL
So you're going to make me wait?

                    REBECCA
Good things come to those who wait.

                    BILL
        (pointing at her)
Friday.

                    REBECCA
        (smiling)
Friday.

Rebecca turns and walks back toward the diner as Bill watches.

INT. BILL'S HOUSE — MORNING

Bill walks into the kitchen whistling. His mom is busy making
an elaborate portrait of an ostrich out of dried macaroni on
red velvet.

                    MOM
You're awfully chipper today.

                    BILL
Chipper?

                    MOM
Yes. Chipper. You know, happy.

                    BILL
No one says chipper anymore.

                    MOM
I can say anything I want. If I want to
call you chipper . . .

                    BILL
All right. I'm chipper.

                    MOM
I suppose you've got another business trip,
don't you? Tonight?

                    BILL
Yep.

                    MOM
I do hope you're getting reimbursed for all
that business you're doing.

                    BILL
Oh, I am. Don't worry.

                    MOM
        (realizing)
Wait a minute . . .

                    BILL
        (worried)
What?

                    MOM
How can you go anywhere? You took your car
in to get fixed.

                    BILL
Yeah, it's Friday. It should be ready
today. If not, I'll get a ride from
somebody at work.

                    MOM
Really? A friend? A female?

                    BILL
Mom.

                    MOM
I'm just interested in your life. Is that a
crime? You never tell me anything.

                    BILL
When there's something to tell, I'll tell
you.

                    MOM
You're sure? I won't have to read about
your wedding in the newspaper, will I?

                    BILL
Have a nice day, Mom.

Bill picks up a dry piece of toast and walks out the back door.

EXT. LENNY'S AUTO BODY SHOP — DAY

Bill walks up to the garage and sees his car waiting outside.
It looks perfect. He approaches the grease monkey working
on another car high in the air. The kid points with a wrench
to his boss, Lenny, who steps out of his office carrying a
clipboard.

                    BILL
The car looks good. You guys did a nice
job.

                    LENNY
Yeah, thanks, we take pride in what we do.
The name's Lenny.

He points to his name embroidered on his stained coveralls. He
flips through pages on his clipboard. Bill notices a centerfold
hanging on a wall.

                    BILL
          I'll be sure to recommend you guys. You own
          the place?

                    LENNY
          I'm the manager. My dad's the owner. If you
          want to step into the office, we can settle
          up.

The two walk into the office. Bill looks around with his arms
folded. He notices an elaborate picture frame sitting on a
desk. The smile is unmistakable: Rebecca. He looks at Lenny,
then back at the picture. He picks it up.

                    LENNY
          Yeah, that's my woman. She's pretty hot,
          isn't she?

Bill puts the picture back down on the desk. He's shaken, but
tries not to show it.

                    LENNY
          What, you don't like women?

                    BILL
          I like women. Sometimes too much.

                    LENNY
          Yeah, I hear ya. If I had my way, I'd be
          fucking 'em all day long. All night too.
          But a guy's got to make a living. Right?

                    BILL
          What do I owe you?

                    LENNY
          Six hundred. But we'll say five-fifty.
          Because I like you.

                    BILL
          All right.

                         LENNY
            So how did you mess up your car?

                         BILL
            You don't want to know.

                         LENNY
            Sure I do. Try me.

                         BILL
            Let's just say there was a woman involved.

Bill keeps looking at the picture.

                         LENNY
            Yeah, cars and women, they'll always give
            you trouble. Here, sign this.

Bill signs absently.

                         LENNY
            Me, I'd rather stick with cars. The only
            problem is . . . you can't fuck your car.
            Am I right?

                         BILL
            I never thought about it that way.

                         LENNY
            I know what I'm talking about. Hey, one
            piece of advice — never trust a woman who
            doesn't respect cars. Here you go.

Lenny hands Bill the receipt.

                         BILL
            Thanks.

Bill gets in his car and drives off slowly.

EXT. BILL'S HOUSE — DAY

Bill parks in the driveway and gets out of his car. He looks at
the damaged area. It's flawless. He walks into the house.

INT. BILL'S HOUSE — DAY

Bill enters his room and sits staring at the door to his
closet. Finally he gets up, walks to the door and opens it with
the hidden key. He steps in and takes a plain wooden box from a
shelf. It's one of dozens of similar boxes.

He opens the lid and stares at the contents for a long moment.
Then he closes the lid and curls up in the corner with the box
clutched to his chest. He looks empty, desperate. He waits a
long moment, then closes his eyes.

EXT. RESTAURANT — DUSK

Rebecca stands waiting, leaning up against her car in her
waitress uniform. Bill pulls up in his car.

                    REBECCA
          Hey, you got it fixed. Nice.

                    BILL
          Yeah. Get in.

                    REBECCA
          Looks good as new.

                    BILL
          Get in.

Rebecca gets in and Bill starts driving, faster than usual.

                    BILL
          You're not wearing your ring.

                    REBECCA
          Yeah I am.

Rebecca unzips the top of her uniform and twists in her seat to
show him. The ring hangs over her heart on a silver chain.

                    BILL
          Okay. You're not wearing a bra.

                    REBECCA
          What are you, my dad?

She zips up. They drive in silence for a while.

                    REBECCA
          What's wrong?

                    BILL
          Nothing.

                    REBECCA
          You're lying.

                    BILL
          Why would I lie?

                    REBECCA
          Fine. Don't tell me.

Rebecca opens the glove compartment and starts searching
through it.

                    BILL
          What are you doing?

                    REBECCA
          Looking for trouble.

                    BILL
          Stop that. I mean it.

                    REBECCA
          What's this?

Rebecca pulls out a small notebook.

                    BILL
          Put that back.

                    REBECCA
               (opening it)
          What the hell? Poetry? You write poetry?

                    BILL
          Yeah. So what?

                              REBECCA
          My God. I suppose you like needlepoint and
          baking cookies.

                                BILL
          You're very judgmental. You know that?

                              REBECCA
          Poetry. Jesus H. Christ.

Rebecca flips through the pages.

                                BILL
          Come on, put it back.

                              REBECCA
          Hey, is this one about me? "My Rebecca"?

Bill looks at her but does not answer.

                              REBECCA
               (reading)
          She's no sunnybrook farm,
          No angel sent from above,
          With white-winged gossamer charm,
          This girl-child grown beyond love.

                                BILL
          Put it back, okay?

                              REBECCA
          No one's ever written a poem about me
          before.

                                BILL
          There's more. Another stanza.

Rebecca turns the page.

                              REBECCA
               (reading)
          Sainted by sin, or tonic and gin,
          Raptures of pleasure and grace,
          She'll take you down with a grin,
          All of your soul laid to waste.

Rebecca stares ahead at the road.

> REBECCA
> I don't know what to say.

> BILL
> It's not finished . . .

> REBECCA
> Thank you.

Rebecca looks away. She's almost crying. Bill looks over at her, surprised by her reaction.

> BILL
> You're welcome.

> REBECCA
> Can I keep it?

> BILL
> Sure. Go ahead.

Rebecca carefully tears out the pages, folds them and puts them in her pocket. She draws a deep breath and resumes her search of the glove compartment.

> REBECCA
> What else you got in here? Are these flares?

> BILL
> No. Careful with those.

> REBECCA
> Fireworks?

> BILL
> No. That's dynamite.

> REBECCA
> What? Are you serious?

> BILL
> Yeah. Light a match and boom.

> REBECCA
>
> Wow. Cool. Give me your matches.

> BILL
>
> No, I don't think so.

> REBECCA
>
> Oh, come on. Please?

> BILL
>
> I've been saving those sticks for a special occasion.

> REBECCA
>
> This is a special occasion. We're celebrating our wedded bliss. Now give me the fucking matches.

Bill gives her the matches.

> BILL
>
> Let me guess. You're planning to launch one out the window.

> REBECCA
>
> Damn straight.

> BILL
>
> Just be good and careful. If you light one of those things and drop it, we're both dead.

> REBECCA
>
> You worry too much.

Rebecca lights and launches a stick. A few seconds later, an explosion goes off behind them.

> REBECCA
>
> Fuck, that felt good. Pull over.

> BILL
>
> What for?

                 REBECCA
I need a better view. Pull over.

Bill pulls over to the shoulder of the road.

EXT. COUNTRY HIGHWAY — DUSK

Bill and Rebecca step out of the car. Bill joins her at the
passenger side. Rebecca lights another stick and throws it. An
explosion rocks the ground forty feet away.

                 REBECCA
Nice. That is so nice.

She lights the last one, but holds it too long.

                 BILL
Now! Throw!

A blast goes off in the air. They both cower from it, huddling
together. They part from each other slowly.

                 BILL
You have a death wish, don't you?

                 REBECCA
Yeah, so? What's your point?

                 BILL
My point is . . . it's not healthy. Trust
me on that.

                 REBECCA
Relax. Breathe.
      (she draws a deep breath)
Enjoy the moment.

                 BILL
If you say so.

                 REBECCA
Fuck, this is so cool. You are the best.

                 BILL
Yeah.

                    REBECCA
No, I mean it. You are the strangest guy
I ever met. You write poetry and you rob
banks and burn down shit and blow up shit.
Christ, it's like we're soulmates.

                     BILL
          (smiling at her)
I know.

                    REBECCA
          (pulling at his shirt)
You just need to loosen up a little.

                     BILL
I'm trying. Believe me.

                    REBECCA
You got any more? More sticks?

                     BILL
Not tonight.

                    REBECCA
This is so cool. You are so cool.

                     BILL
I'm glad you like it.

                    REBECCA
Hey, we could use these to rob a bank. Make
some nice big motherfuckin' holes.

                     BILL
What? Just walk in and throw dynamite around?

                    REBECCA
Sure, why not?

                     BILL
Well, for one thing, it's completely
unnecessary. You can walk in and say you
have dynamite and they'll take your word
for it. They'll give you the money. You
don't have to ruin anyone's day by blowing
them up.

                    REBECCA
          (pouting)
     Fine. But I still want to blow up
     <u>something</u>.

                    BILL
     Yeah, well, it's not my ambition in life to
     be a bank robber.

                    REBECCA
     You did it before.

                    BILL
     I told you, I'm not robbing a bank.

                    REBECCA
     Okay, fine.

She looks at him with clear annoyance and frustration.

                    REBECCA
     But we can still blow up something.
     Sometime. Right?

                    BILL
     Maybe.
          (pause)
     You have to answer me one question.

                    REBECCA
     Okay. Shoot.

                    BILL
     Why?

                    REBECCA
     What?

                    BILL
     The reason you want to blow up the planet.
     I want to know why.

                    REBECCA
     I don't want to blow up the planet. Just
     part of it.

                    BILL
All right. Why?

                    REBECCA
Do I need a reason?

                    BILL
No. Just asking if you have one.
     (pause)
You do, don't you?

                    REBECCA
I don't know. Maybe.

                    BILL
Tell me.

                    REBECCA
I never told anybody.

                    BILL
I'm not anybody.
     (pause)
Was it your dad?

                    REBECCA
No. My mom.

                    BILL
What about her?

                    REBECCA
She used to beat on me. With a big wooden
spoon. Never my older brothers, just me. I
can still hear her voice screaming my name.
She fucking hated me.

                    BILL
What was her problem?

                    REBECCA
Hell, I don't know. My dad said she had
some kind of mental thing. I haven't seen
her in years.

                    BILL
        Is she getting help?

                    REBECCA
        Help? This is America. People don't get
        help. They get screwed.

                    BILL
            (smirking)
        That's not very patriotic.

                    REBECCA
        Yeah, fuck that.

                    BILL
            (grinning)
        Hey now, if you don't love America, you
        must be some kind of terrorist.

                    REBECCA
        Yeah. You want to see terror, I can show
        you terror.

Rebecca moves closer to Bill in a menacing way.

                    BILL
        I'm not afraid of you.

                    REBECCA
            (crossing her arms)
        Oh really?

                    BILL
        Okay, maybe a little.

                    REBECCA
        Good. You're not as dumb as you look.

Rebecca snuggles up to him, kissing him hard. Then she pulls
away.

                    REBECCA
        Hey, guess what? I got you something.

She reaches in her pocket and hands him a large rounded metal
ring.

                    BILL
          Um, thanks. I don't think it's going to
          fit . . .

                    REBECCA
          You don't wear it on your hand.

                    BILL
          Then where? On my foot?

                    REBECCA
          No. Think again.

                    BILL
               (thinks a moment)
          Oh.

                    REBECCA
               (smiles wickedly)
          With this ring . . . I thee fuck.

Rebecca throws herself at him.

INT. HOTEL — NIGHT

Bill is alone, lounging in a robe, staring out the window. He's
holding a tiny bottle of alcohol from the minibar. He checks
his watch. The TV is playing a tornado documentary with no
sound.

Rebecca walks in and slams the door behind her. She's wearing
her black baseball cap with the Circle J logo.

                    REBECCA
          You _fucking_ mother fucker.

                    BILL
          What?

                    REBECCA
          You lied to me.

                    BILL
What are you talking about?

                    REBECCA
You fucking lied. You didn't rob a bank.

                    BILL
Wait a minute . . .

                    REBECCA
Admit it. Just fucking admit it. You think
I'm stupid. Just some stupid little bitch
you can fuck with.

                    BILL
No. That's not . . . no.

                    REBECCA
I checked the web. Jackson has a newspaper,
you know. That town hasn't had a bank
robbed in over a year. A full goddamned
year.

                    BILL
I gave you the money.

                    REBECCA
Yeah, forty-five hundred. Just where the
hell did you get that?

                    BILL
What's the big deal? Money is money.

                    REBECCA
I only asked you for one thing. For you to
be straight with me.

                    BILL
Okay. Fine. I went to Jackson. I had
everything ready. But I couldn't do it. I
wanted to. But I didn't.

                    REBECCA
Great. That's just great. I knew it. Fuck
you. That's why you said you didn't want to

rob any more banks. Because you never did
it in the first place. So where'd you get
the money?

                    BILL
What does it matter? You said it yourself,
money's the only thing that counts.
Everything else is bullshit.

Rebecca pulls out her switchblade and pops it open.

                    REBECCA
Tell me right now or I swear I'll cut you.

                    BILL
        (putting his hands up)
Okay . . . I took it . . .

                    REBECCA
From where?

                    BILL
My . . . savings account.

                    REBECCA
What the fuck?

                    BILL
You wanted to see a pile of money.
So . . .

                    REBECCA
Oh Christ.

Rebecca flings the knife to the floor in disgust.

                    BILL
I didn't know what else to do.

                    REBECCA
I don't fucking believe it. I really don't.

She starts pacing back and forth.

                    BILL
I'm sorry. Okay?

                    REBECCA
          Christ. This is great. How the hell did I
          hook up with somebody like you?

                    BILL
          I don't know. I guess you just got lucky.

                    REBECCA
          Shut up. Just shut the hell up.

                    BILL
          Okay.

                    REBECCA
          So I am a fucking prostitute. You never
          robbed a bank. You gave me forty-five
          hundred dollars. Just to have sex with me.

                    BILL
          Yeah I did. But it was worth it.

Rebecca cocks her hand on her hip. She stares at Bill, trying
to decide if he's incredibly sweet or incredibly stupid.

                    REBECCA
          What the hell am I going to do with you?

                    BILL
          I have a suggestion.

Rebecca takes off her cap and puts it on him. She steps back
to admire the look. She's turned him into herself, into her
father. Rebecca moves closer to Bill and smiles.

                    REBECCA
          I owe you this.

Rebecca lands a sucker punch in Bill's gut. He doubles over in
pain. He tries to stay standing but drops to his knees.

                    BILL
              (breathless)
          Fuck. That hurt.

>   REBECCA
>   Yeah. Remember, this is how it feels.

>   BILL
>   Christ. You've got an arm.

>   REBECCA
>   That's rule number one. Don't mess with a
>   badass. Got that?

>   BILL
>   Got it.

Rebecca kneels and brings her face close to his.

>   REBECCA
>   (smiling)
>   You lie to me again . . . I swear I'll
>   fucking kill you.

>   BILL
>   You got a deal.

She pushes him to the floor, then jumps on top of him, pulling off his robe, kissing him like crazy.

INT. BILL'S HOUSE — DAY

Mom is working on an abstract oil painting in the living room. She hears noises coming from the hallway.

>   MOM
>   Bill? Is that you? Where are you going? I
>   want to know. You're never home anymore.
>   I'm beginning to think you don't like me.

Bill walks into the room. He's dressed for work in a white shirt and thin black tie.

>   BILL
>   You know I love you, Mom.

>   MOM
>   Yes, that's very sweet. But I never get to
>   see you these days. You've got a girl, I
>   know it. Am I right?

                    BILL
         See you later.

                    MOM
         You can bring her around. I would love to
         meet her, you know. What's her name?

Bill leaves with a wave.

EXT. PICNIC SITE — AFTERNOON

Lying on a blanket on the grass, Rebecca and Bill stare up
at the sky. A tall water tower stands nearby. A row of trees
offers some privacy from the road. Bill looks over at Rebecca.
She's half dressed.

                    BILL
         Damn it.

                    REBECCA
         What?

                    BILL
         There's just something about you.

                    REBECCA
         Yeah. I know.

                    BILL
         Something . . . I can't put my finger on
         it.

                    REBECCA
              (with a naughty smile)
         Sure you can. Go ahead.

                    BILL
         Is everything about sex?

                    REBECCA
         Sex is good. Sex is fun. Sex is your
         friend.

                    BILL
         Sex is a weapon. A bomb waiting to blow up
         in your face.

Rebecca moves closer and looks at him mischievously.

> BILL
> Tick. Tick.

> REBECCA
> Boom.

She kisses him, briefly, sweetly.

> BILL
> It's weird, I feel like I've known you
> forever. It's like we're connected.

> REBECCA
>   (smirks)
> Not at the moment.

> BILL
> No, I mean the person inside there.
>   (he taps on her forehead)
> Inside that head of yours.

> REBECCA
> Oh, you don't want to go there.

> BILL
> Too late.

Rebecca stands and plucks Bill's gun from his jacket lying on
the hood of his car. She takes aim and fires off a shot at the
water tower nearby. The bullet ricochets off with a sharp PING.

> BILL
> What the hell? Stop that.

> REBECCA
> I want to see it take a leak.

> BILL
> Yeah, well, that's not going to work. The
> metal's too thick. You need a high-powered
> rifle. Maybe even a special kind of bullet.
> That gun is only good for putting holes in
> people.

                    REBECCA
But what if I want to do some serious
damage?

                    BILL
Then you need to get serious.

                    REBECCA
And what does that mean?

                    BILL
You need the right tools. There's an
instruction book you can read. The
Anarchist Cookbook.

                    REBECCA
The what?

                    BILL
Anarchist. Like anarchy. You know, no
rules.

                    REBECCA
So you got a copy? I want one.

                    BILL
The government doesn't like people to have
copies. They think folks might do bad
things.

                    REBECCA
Do you have one? Yes or no?

                    BILL
You're dangerous.

                    REBECCA
Oh, you have no idea.

Bill takes the gun from her and puts it back in his jacket.
Rebecca sits down on the grass. Bill folds his arms and stands
staring at her.

                    BILL
        You know, one of these days, stuff might
        just catch up with you.

                    REBECCA
        What stuff?

                    BILL
        You think you can do anything. Anything
        you want. Anything that enters that pretty
        little head.

                    REBECCA
        Yeah. Why not?

Bill sits down next to her.

                    BILL
        Well, for one thing, the police. They might
        not like it if you go around shooting up
        the town.

                    REBECCA
        Fuck the police. No one tells me what I can
        do.

                    BILL
        Whatever you say.

                    REBECCA
        Damn straight. I don't take shit from no
        one. Never have, never will.

                    BILL
        Yeah. Okay.

Bill reaches over and rubs Rebecca's shoulders. She closes her
eyes.

                    REBECCA
        Do me one favor.

                    BILL
        Maybe.

> REBECCA
Get me some more of those big sticks.

Bill smiles and closes his eyes.

INT. HOTEL — NIGHT

Bill and Rebecca lie in bed. They open their eyes at almost the same time.

> REBECCA
Why are we here?

> BILL
On this planet?

> REBECCA
No. Here. In this hotel. Why do we keep coming here?

> BILL
I like it.

> REBECCA
Okay. Why not your place?

> BILL
I told you, I like it here.

> REBECCA
What, are you married?

> BILL
You want to know the truth?

> REBECCA
Yeah, I do.

> BILL
You sure?

> REBECCA
Yes. Damn it.

                    BILL
          I'm not married. It's just . . . me and my
          mom. We share the same house.

Rebecca pulls away from him.

                    REBECCA
          Jesus Christ. Are you kidding me? Your
          mother? You live with your mother?

                    BILL
          What's wrong with that?

                    REBECCA
          How old are you?

                    BILL
          She needs me.

                    REBECCA
          What, is she some kind of invalid?

                    BILL
          No.

                    REBECCA
          Then what?

                    BILL
          I care about my mother. Is that so wrong?

                    REBECCA
              (shaking her head)
          Jesus. A badass who writes poetry and lives
          with his mommy. That's just great.

Rebecca gets out of bed and starts putting on her clothes.

                    BILL
          Okay, so I'm not a badass. Not the kind
          you're used to. Bunch of knuckle-scraping
          losers.

REBECCA

Any one of them could kick your ass. That's
for damn sure. Hell, I could kick your ass.

BILL

Why don't we just forget this?

REBECCA

Forget what?

BILL

This. All of this. You and me. Us. It's no
good.

REBECCA

Really?

BILL

Really. You're not my type anyway.

REBECCA

What? Not your type? What the hell does
that mean?

BILL

You're blonde.

REBECCA

So?

BILL

I like women with dark hair. The darker the
better. Black is best.

REBECCA

Why? What's so great about dark hair?

BILL

Hell, I don't know. It's just a thing.

REBECCA

There has to be a reason. You have to know
why.

                        BILL
          No I don't. I told you, it's just a thing.
          My mom had blonde hair. Now it's gray.

Rebecca sits down on the bed. She stares at her hands for a
long moment.

                      REBECCA
          I could dye my hair.

                        BILL
          No. Don't do that.

Bill moves next to Rebecca and holds her in a gentle, fatherly
way. At first she stiffens, then she relaxes and lets herself
be held. Bill nuzzles her hair.

                        BILL
          It's like I can see inside you. The person
          who hurts, who feels everything too much,
          doubts everyone, herself included.

                      REBECCA
          Shut up.

                        BILL
          You deserve to be loved. Properly.

                      REBECCA
          No.

She breaks away from him and moves to the window, staring out
at the darkness. Bill stands.

                        BILL
          You keep getting fucked over. So many times
          now you think it's right. Well, I've got
          news, it's never going to be right. Your
          life is going to suck right up until the
          moment you decide to change it. And if you
          never do, then God help you.

                      REBECCA
          What the hell are you talking about? How
          fucked up do you think I am?

                    BILL
I know you have a boyfriend.

                  REBECCA
What?

                    BILL
Don't deny it. I know it's true.

                  REBECCA
Have you been following me? Spying on me?

                    BILL
No. I got my car fixed. By a guy named
Lenny. He seems like a real asshole.

                  REBECCA
He's not an asshole. Okay?

                    BILL
Yeah. If you say so.

                  REBECCA
It's not like I'm married to him or
anything. I have my own place.

                    BILL
You don't have to explain.

                  REBECCA
Fine. I won't.

Rebecca waits for Bill to say something. He doesn't.

                  REBECCA
So now what? Is this a problem?

                    BILL
          (thinks a moment)
I'm not happy about it.

                  REBECCA
I didn't ask if you were happy. I asked if
we have a problem. Well? Do we?

                        BILL
              (thinks a long moment)
        No. We don't. We're good.

                      REBECCA
        Really? You sure about that?

                        BILL
        Yeah. I'm sure. Except for one small thing.

                      REBECCA
        What's that?

                        BILL
        You lied to me.

                      REBECCA
        I didn't <u>lie</u> . . .

                        BILL
        Call it what you want. You didn't tell me
        the truth. You could have been honest with
        me.

                      REBECCA
        What about you? You lied right in my face.
        You said you robbed a bank.

                        BILL
        Okay. Yeah. Fine, I lied.

                      REBECCA
        Damn straight.

                        BILL
        Look, whatever. No more lying. No more
        secrets. Okay? From now on.

                      REBECCA
        Fine.

Rebecca sits down on the bed. Bill sits next to her.

                        BILL
        So how do we get rid of Lenny?

                    REBECCA
What?

                    BILL
Does he have life insurance? He could have
an accident.

                    REBECCA
Very funny.

                    BILL
I'm just saying, accidents happen.

                    REBECCA
Shut up.

                    BILL
What do you see in that guy?

                    REBECCA
He can be nice. Sometimes.
     (pause)
Did you tell him? About us? Does he know?

                    BILL
No. I didn't say a word.

                    REBECCA
Good.
     (pause)
So what about you? You have a girlfriend on
the side?

                    BILL
No. Not unless you count my mom.

                    REBECCA
What?

                    BILL
I'm kidding. Look, let's not worry about
anyone else. When it's just you and me,
that's all there is. Okay?

                    REBECCA
That could work. I suppose.

> BILL
>> Starting now. It's just you and me, babe.

Rebecca smiles at his attempt to be suave.

> REBECCA
>> Christ, you're such a fucking idiot.

Bill leans close to her. Rebecca rests her head on his shoulder.

INT. BILL'S KITCHEN — MORNING

Bill catches a slice of toast as it pops out of the toaster. Mom works on a painting in a sunny corner. Bill sits down at the table. Mom joins him. She notices the Circle J cap lying on the table. She picks it up, then quickly puts it back down.

> MOM
>> The Circle J? When did you go there?

> BILL
>> The other night.

> MOM
>> Well, it's a small world.

Bill is about to take a sip of his coffee but stops himself. He does not want to ask . . .

> BILL
>> What do you mean?

> MOM
>> Your father and I used to go there. It was called the Colonnade back then. It was such a nice place in those days. Great food. Very classy. And now it's a biker bar, isn't it? You shouldn't go there.

> BILL
>> It's not dangerous. Don't worry.

                    MOM
        It used to be beautiful. I was so
        disappointed when Jimbo bought it and
        changed the name.

Mom picks up the cap again. Bill looks uneasy as he watches her
pull a long blonde hair from inside.

                    BILL
        Jimbo? You know him?

                    MOM
        Oh yes. We go way back. Is he still there?

                    BILL
        Yeah, he's the bartender. Packs a gun. You
        know Jimbo?

                    MOM
        Yes. Your father never got along with
        Jimmy. Always called him the black sheep.

                    BILL
        What do you mean . . . black sheep?

                    MOM
        The black sheep of the family. Jimbo's my
        brother. Haven't seen him in ages now. Must
        be almost twenty years. Or more.

                    BILL
        Brother?

Mom nods, staring out the window now.

                    BILL
        Mom . . . you never mentioned anything
        about . . . I mean, you're kidding, right?

                    MOM
        No. Is something wrong? You don't look so
        good.

                    BILL
        No, I'm fine.

                    (takes a deep breath)
          You're saying Jimbo is my uncle?

                         MOM
          As I say, it's a small world.

Mom stares at the cap then puts it on Bill's head. She leaves
the room. After a few seconds, he takes it off and holds it
over his heart.

INT. BILL'S OFFICE — DAY

Bill sits at his desk, shuffling papers absently. He stops,
closes his eyes and takes a deep breath. He shakes his head,
then resumes his work.

EXT. DINER PARKING LOT — NIGHT

Bill checks his watch and waits, leaning against the side of
his car. The lights inside the diner go dark. Then the lighted
sign goes dark. Rebecca walks out from the shadows and sees
Bill. Their two cars are the last in the lot.

                       REBECCA
          What's wrong?

                         BILL
          Nothing.

                       REBECCA
          You look like it's the end of the world.

                         BILL
          No, I'm fine.

                       REBECCA
          Tell me. Don't make me hurt you.

                         BILL
          Okay. Look, I swear I did not try to
          get this information. Your last name, is
          it . . . Jenkins?

Rebecca glares at Bill. She's clearly pissed off.

                    BILL
Your dad, his name is Jim Jenkins? The guy
who runs the Circle J? Am I right?

                    REBECCA
Yeah. So what?

                    BILL
Jesus.

                    REBECCA
What?

                    BILL
My last name . . .

                    REBECCA
Look, names don't matter. I told you that.

                    BILL
Yes, they do matter.

Bill reaches for his wallet, pulls out his driver's license and
hands it to her.

                    REBECCA
Nice mustache. Hey, you're younger than
me . . .

                    BILL
Look at the name.

                    REBECCA
Bill.
     (in a softer voice)
Jenkins.

                    BILL
Your dad . . . and my mom . . . are brother
and sister.

                    REBECCA
Okay. So that makes us . . .

                    BILL
Cousins. We're first cousins.

                        REBECCA
No way.

                         BILL
My mom just told me. I don't know, for
some reason, our fathers, they never got
along. Shit, I never even knew my mom had a
brother. Or that I had . . . you.

                        REBECCA
We're cousins? Fuckin' cousins?

                         BILL
Yeah.

                        REBECCA
        (laughs)
That's a hoot.

Rebecca starts kissing him passionately, rubbing her hands all
over him.

                         BILL
Wait. Stop. We can't do this.

                        REBECCA
Why not?

                         BILL
You know why. We have the same last name.

                        REBECCA
So? I don't care.

                         BILL
You should care. It's not right.

                        REBECCA
Fuck that.

                         BILL
But . . . we're related to each other.

                        REBECCA
        (shrugs)
Yeah, it's weird. What are the odds?

Rebecca goes back in for a kiss. Bill holds her off.

                    BILL
          Don't you get it? We're <u>related</u> to each
          other.

                    REBECCA
          Yeah. You said that. Big deal. The whole
          planet is related to each other. What does
          it matter?

                    BILL
          I don't know, it just feels . . . wrong.

                    REBECCA
          Wrong can be good. Really good. Or haven't
          you figured that out yet?

                    BILL
          Um, I don't know . . .

                    REBECCA
          I don't see any problem. Do you?

Rebecca unzips the front of her uniform, revealing too much
flesh.

                    BILL
          Well . . .

                    REBECCA
          Good. I thought so.

Rebecca starts to go at him, nuzzling his neck.

                    BILL
          Stop. Don't.
               (weaker)
          Stop.
               (a whisper)
          Please.

EXT. BILL'S HOUSE — DAY

Bill is loading the trunk of his car with wooden boxes, the
same boxes that were in his closet. Rebecca is sitting in the
passenger seat. She's reading a book of poetry by Sylvia Plath.

Mom walks out from around the side of the house. She's wearing
a wide-brimmed straw hat and carrying pruning shears. She
watches Bill for a few seconds as he moves boxes.

                    MOM
          What are you doing?

Rebecca quickly ducks down in the seat to hide.

                    BILL
          Mom? Why aren't you out with Dolores? Like
          you said?

                    MOM
          She's sick. What are all these boxes?

                    BILL
          I'm just getting rid of some stuff.

                    MOM
          Well, good. I'm glad to see you doing that.
          Something constructive.

Bill smiles at his mom and packs the last of the boxes in the
backseat.

INT. BILL'S CAR — DAY

Bill starts up the car and drives off. As soon as the car
rounds the corner, Rebecca sits up and looks at Bill.

                    REBECCA
          Constructive?

                    BILL
          Yeah.

                    REBECCA
          She doesn't know you at all, does she?

The two smile at each other.

EXT. PICNIC SITE — DAY

Bill and Rebecca are kneeling together about a hundred feet
away from the water tower. Bill is holding a toy remote control
with wires attached. He's staring at the device with a worried
expression.

                    BILL
          I don't know.

                    REBECCA
          Don't know what?

                    BILL
          If this is wrong.

                    REBECCA
          The wiring?

                    BILL
          No. <u>This</u>. Whether this whole thing is
          wrong.

                    REBECCA
          Of course it's wrong. It's against the law.
          It's totally wrong. Your mommy would not
          approve. So what? Do it anyway. That's the
          whole point. Know it's wrong. And <u>do</u> <u>it</u>
          <u>anyway</u>.

                    BILL
          Really? Just like that?

                    REBECCA
          Yeah, just like that. I told you before,
          you've got two choices. You fuck or you
          fuck off. It's that simple.

                    BILL
          Oh yeah?

                    REBECCA
          Yeah. You can be a scared little pig. Or
          you can huff . . . and puff . . . and blow
          it all down.

                    (in a husky whisper)
          Blow it . . . all . . . <u>down</u>.

Bill flips the switch on the remote. Three powerful explosions
rock the base of the water tower.

Bill and Rebecca watch in awe. The sounds of twisting metal
accompany the sight of the swaying tower, now missing three
support legs at its base. Bill and Rebecca realize together
that the thing might land on them if they don't get out of its
way.

They run as fast as they can and the tower crashes down behind,
cracking open and drenching them with a wall of water that
knocks them to the ground.

After a few seconds lying stunned, Bill flicks water from
himself and moves to help Rebecca up.

                         BILL
          You okay?

                       REBECCA
          Yeah, I'm fine. That was fun.

                         BILL
          Yeah, it was a blast.

                       REBECCA
          Do me. Right now.

Rebecca wraps her arm around his neck.

                         BILL
          No, right now we need to get in the car and
          drive.

                       REBECCA
          Please.

Bill takes the time to grab her shoulders and kiss her hard.
Then he takes her hand and runs with her in tow.

EXT. BRIDGE — DAY

Bill's car drives slowly over a bridge and parks near the end.
Bill and Rebecca get out. He leans against the side of the car.
Rebecca is bouncing with joy. Both are still soaking wet.

                    REBECCA
          We did it. I don't believe it. You're for
          real.

                    BILL
          Yeah. So are you.

                    REBECCA
          Of course. But I had my doubts about you.

A police car zooms past with lights flashing and siren wailing.

                    REBECCA
          Gee, I wonder why he's in such a hurry.

                    BILL
          You got me.

                    REBECCA
          This is perfect. I love it. This is so
          perfect.

Rebecca does a little dance. Bill watches her and smiles.

INT. DINER — MORNING

Bill sits at the counter reading a newspaper that prominently
features the demise of the water tower. Lydia approaches with a
pot of coffee.

                    LYDIA
          You again. She's not here.

                    BILL
          Who?

                    LYDIA
          Who do you think? Who else?

                         BILL
                    (smiling)
               My Rebecca.

Bill flips his coffee cup over and Lydia fills it.

                         LYDIA
               So did you read all about the tower?

                         BILL
               Yeah. Boom.

                         LYDIA
               I mean, why the hell would anyone do that?
               It makes no sense.

                         BILL
               There's still one on the other side of
               town. We should be fine. You can still make
               coffee.

                         LYDIA
               Don't look now. Your friend is here.

Lydia walks back to her customers. Rebecca steps close and
takes a seat next to Bill. She's wearing dark glasses.

                         BILL
               There's my water tower girl. What's with
               the glasses?

                         REBECCA
               Nothing.

                         BILL
               Oh Christ. Don't tell me . . .

                         REBECCA
               I got in an argument.

Rebecca takes off the glasses, showing a bruise by her eye.

                         BILL
               Shit.

>   REBECCA
>   He found your poem.

>   BILL
>   Lenny?

>   REBECCA
>   He wasn't happy. He called it a love poem.
>   It's good he didn't see the ring you gave
>   me.

>   BILL
>   Don't worry, I know what to do.

>   REBECCA
>   What?

>   BILL
>   It's simple. I'm going to kill him.

Bill moves to stand but Rebecca grabs his arm and forces him to
sit.

>   REBECCA
>   No. Come on.

>   BILL
>   Why not? Give me one good reason.

>   REBECCA
>   You could end up in jail. I need you.

Bill pauses a moment, impressed by her admission.

>   BILL
>   I'm not going to let him hurt you.

>   REBECCA
>   He won't do it again. He just lost it this
>   time. I don't know why.

>   BILL
>   I know why. He's an asshole.

Rebecca stares at the counter. She does not defend him.

                        BILL
          He's done it before. Hasn't he?

Rebecca puts her glasses back on. She does not answer.

                        BILL
          I can make it look like an accident. His
          little gas station just happens to go up
          in a big ball of flames. And he happens
          to be inside. I can see it. Plain as day.
          Beautiful.

                      REBECCA
          Stop it. I don't want anyone to die.

                        BILL
          Why not? He deserves it.

                      REBECCA
          No. I said no.

                        BILL
                (disappointed)
          Okay. But we need to do something.

                      REBECCA
          Like what?

                        BILL
                (thinks a moment)
          Well, for one thing, we should get out of
          this damned town.

                      REBECCA
          No way. I'm not afraid of him.

                        BILL
          This town is too small. It's not good.

                      REBECCA
          I don't want to run. Not because of some
          guy.

                        BILL
          Look . . .

                         REBECCA
          No. A badass doesn't turn and run.

                         BILL
          And a badass doesn't put up with shit like
          that.

Bill gestures to her face.

                         REBECCA
          Thanks. Thanks a lot.

                         BILL
          No, look, I didn't mean it like that. What
          I'm trying to say . . . it's better if we
          leave. There's Lenny. And there's my mom.
          It's too much. We can't just stay here and
          live together. Happily ever after.

Rebecca takes off her glasses.

                         REBECCA
          Wait a minute. Are you saying you want to
          live together? Like real people? You want
          to be my boyfriend?

                         BILL
          I'm saying we should get away. Start fresh.
          Forget everything here.

                         REBECCA
          Answer the question. Yes or no. Do you want
          to be my boyfriend?

                         BILL
          I'm your husband. Remember?

                         REBECCA
          Yeah. But do you want to be my boyfriend?

There's a long pause as Rebecca and Bill stare at each other.

                         BILL
          It's all I think about. Every second of the
          day.

                         REBECCA
          And night?

Bill takes Rebecca's hand and smiles.

INT. BILL'S HOUSE — DUSK

Bill and Rebecca enter cautiously through the front door. She's
wearing her dark glasses and carrying an army duffel bag. They
quietly enter the living room. Hearing the sound of dishes,
they move toward the kitchen and slowly step inside.

                         BILL
          Hey Mom. This is a friend of mine.

                         MOM
          Oh. My. Hello there. It's nice to meet you.

Mom looks Rebecca up and down, then returns to clanking dishes.

                         MOM
          So, are you two an item?

                         BILL
          We're friends, Mom. All right?

                         MOM
               (puts down her dishes)
          I'm just asking. Please, come on in, sit
          down. Can I get you something?

                         BILL
          Mom, here's the thing. Rebecca needs a
          place to stay for a while. I told her she
          could stay here.

                         MOM
               (blinks a few times)
          Oh. Of course. Sure. Why not?

                         REBECCA
          Thank you.

                    MOM
Certainly. We have an extra bedroom. You
two aren't sleeping together, are you?

                    BILL
Mom, I told you, we're friends.

                    MOM
All right, Billy, don't get all excited.

                    REBECCA
        (smiling at him)
Billy.

                    MOM
Make yourself at home. Please. Our house is
your house.

                    REBECCA
Thank you. I appreciate it.

Rebecca looks uncertain. Mom looks uncomfortable.

                    BILL
Come on. I'll show you the room.

Bill and Rebecca leave the kitchen and head upstairs.

                    REBECCA
Are you sure this is okay?

                    BILL
Sure, what do you mean?

                    REBECCA
Me being here. It feels weird.

                    BILL
You'll get used to it.

                    REBECCA
I'm not exactly the kind of girl you take
home to mother.

                    BILL
               (smiles)
          Too late.

Bill opens the door to the spare bedroom. It's decorated in
pastel fabrics and flowery art. Rebecca looks around and tosses
her bag on the bed.

                    REBECCA
          This is nice. Very quaint. Like the home I
          never had.

                    BILL
          It might be a bit dusty.

                    REBECCA
          I don't mind. Where's your room?

                    BILL
          Over here. Across the hall.

Bill opens the door to his room and steps inside, tossing his
jacket on a chair. Rebecca steps in and looks around in awe at
the spare black and white décor.

                    REBECCA
          Wow. You live in here?

                    BILL
          Yeah.

                    REBECCA
          It's weird.

                    BILL
          Yeah.

                    REBECCA
          I like it.
               (pause)
          Where's that book you were talking about?
          The one about how to do bad shit.

                    BILL
          No. I don't think so.

                    REBECCA
        Oh, come on. You promised.

                    BILL
        I think we've caused enough damage already.

                    REBECCA
        Not at all. We're just getting started.

Bill moves closer to Rebecca, both eyeing each other with a
steady gaze. When Bill reaches her, he grabs under her arms and
lifts her in the air. Mom suddenly appears in the doorway.

                    MOM
        Oh, I'm sorry.

Bill quickly puts Rebecca back down on the floor. She
straightens her shirt.

                    BILL
        We were just playing.

                    MOM
        Towels. Clean towels are in the dryer. Just
        finished.

Mom leaves in a hurry. Bill and Rebecca smile at each other,
trying not to laugh.

INT. KITCHEN — MORNING

Mom and Rebecca sit at the kitchen table eating breakfast.
Rebecca is not wearing her glasses and the bruise is apparent.

                    MOM
        Tell me. Who did this to you? I need to
        know. Certainly not my Billy.

                    REBECCA
        No. Not Billy.

                    MOM
        Who then?

                    REBECCA
My boyfriend. Ex-boyfriend.

                    MOM
Did you go to the police?

                    REBECCA
No.

                    MOM
So that's why you're staying here. To get
away. My God. You can stay here as long as
you like. If you want me to hurt him, I
will. I know people. Oh hell, I can do it
myself.

                    REBECCA
     (smiles sheepishly)
Thanks.

                    MOM
You look so much like a little girl.
     (realizes)
Oh dear Lord.

                    REBECCA
What?

                    MOM
Your face. Your eyes.

                    REBECCA
What about 'em?

                    MOM
You're . . . Rebecca. Becky!

                    REBECCA
Yeah. So?

                    MOM
Becky Jenkins. Do you know who you are?

                    REBECCA
Yeah. Sometimes.

MOM

I haven't seen you since . . . since
you were a child. Four years old. You're
my . . . my niece.

Rebecca smiles weakly and looks down at her hands.

MOM

Why didn't you say something? Did you know?
You're Bill's cousin.

REBECCA
(defensively)
We're friends. We just met a little while
ago.

MOM

Oh my God. It is such a small world.

REBECCA

I guess.

MOM

How's your father doing?

REBECCA

He's okay. Still the same guy.

MOM

I don't believe it. Billy should have said
something. He was asking me about the
Circle J and I never realized. My goodness,
look at you. You're a grown woman.

Bill appears in the doorway in his pajamas, his hair rumpled.

BILL

Mom, what are you doing?

MOM

We're talking. It's not a crime.

REBECCA

She knows.

                    BILL
Knows what?

                    MOM
That this is Becky. Rebecca. Your cousin.

                    BILL
Oh. Right. I was going to mention that.

                    MOM
Billy, you don't have to keep things from
me. Why wouldn't you tell me this? I'm your
mother. We're all family here.

                    BILL
Yeah. Tell me about it.

                    MOM
Well, one thing is settled.
          (looks at Rebecca)
You will stay here as long as you like.
I will not allow you to be man-handled by
some good-for-nothing boyfriend.
          (looks away)
You're family.

Mom goes to the sink and finds only a trickle of water from the
tap. Bill sits.

                    MOM
Damn it. Will you look at this? Almost no
water. Just a trickle. All because of some
stupid kids.

                    BILL
Kids?

                    MOM
Yes. Didn't you hear? Some idiot kids
managed to knock down the water tower. So
now everyone has to pay the price.

                    BILL
          (shakes his head)
Yeah, kids these days.

Rebecca and Bill exchange looks.

>   MOM
>   One thing I know for sure — people don't
>   know how to raise children anymore. The
>   acorn doesn't fall far from the tree.
>   That's what your father used to say.

Bill and Rebecca smile at each other. She rubs her feet against his under the table.

EXT. COUNTRY ROAD — DAY

Bill leans up against the side of his car, waiting. Lenny pulls up in his red tow truck. He gets out of the truck and approaches Bill.

>   LENNY
>   So, what seems to be the problem?

Lenny waits for an answer but Bill just stares at him.

>   LENNY
>   With your <u>car</u>?

>   BILL
>   There's nothing wrong with the car. The
>   problem is you.

>   LENNY
>   What? I came out here to tow a car.

>   BILL
>   I lied. The car's fine.

>   LENNY
>   Great. Thanks a lot. Why the hell did you
>   call for a tow?

>   BILL
>   I need a word with you.

>   LENNY
>   A word?

                    BILL
Rebecca.

                    LENNY
What about her? You know her?

                    BILL
She's a friend of mine.

                    LENNY
Yeah. So?

                    BILL
I don't like it when friends of mine get
hurt.

                    LENNY
Yeah, well, it's really none of your
business.

                    BILL
        (with a twisted smile)
Oh, I'm afraid it is my business.

                    LENNY
Wait. I get it now. You're the guy who
wrote the poem. The love poem. Am I right?

Lenny waits for an answer but Bill offers no reply.

                    LENNY
And you brought me out here because you
wanna play the tough guy? Right?

                    BILL
No. I don't want to play anything.

                    LENNY
Then what?

                    BILL
        (speaking slowly)
Listen very carefully. If you touch her
again, if you even think about touching
her, you will suffer long and hard. Right
before you die.

                    LENNY
So you're threatening me? That's real nice.

                    BILL
No. No threat. This is a solemn oath before
God. I will kill you. I will gladly fucking
kill you. It will make me so very happy to
end your life. And it will make the world a
much better place.

                    LENNY
You think you can scare me?

                    BILL
     (smiling)
You just don't understand, do you?

                    LENNY
Oh, I understand . . .

Bill pulls out a gun, points it at Lenny's head for a few
seconds, then moves it just slightly to the left and fires.
Lenny drops, covering his head.

                    LENNY
What the hell? You're out of your fucking
mind!

                    BILL
Very good. Now you understand. I am out of
my fucking mind.

Bill pulls out a second gun and levels it at Lenny.

                    BILL
And I will gladly kill you. If you ever
disappoint me.

Lenny gets back in his truck, spins it around and drives off.
Bill keeps his guns leveled at the truck as it speeds away.

EXT. BILL'S HOUSE — DAY

Bill pulls up in his car and gets out. He sees Rebecca in the backyard lounging in the sun in a bikini top and denim shorts. She's reading another book.

>   REBECCA
>   Hey. What's wrong? Where were you?

>   BILL
>   Just taking care of business. I had a
>   little chat . . . with Lenny.

>   REBECCA
>   What? Really? You didn't kill him, did you?

>   BILL
>   No. I just gave him something to think
>   about. Which reminds me, I got you
>   something.

Bill pulls a gun from his jacket and offers it to Rebecca. She stands and takes it.

>   REBECCA
>   Are you serious? You're giving me a gun?

>   BILL
>   Yeah. I still have mine.

>   REBECCA
>   Okay. But . . . what's it for?

>   BILL
>   For shooting people. You know how to shoot.
>   I've seen you.

>   REBECCA
>   Yeah, I can pull a trigger.

>   BILL
>   Just be careful, it's loaded.

Rebecca points the gun at the trunk of a thick oak tree but Bill forces her to lower the weapon.

                         BILL
      Don't do that.

                         REBECCA
      What, are you a tree-hugger?

                         BILL
      Yeah. I am.

                         REBECCA
      Me too.

Rebecca stares down at the gun in her hand. She looks worried.

                         BILL
      Relax. Breathe.

Rebecca smiles weakly.

INT. DINING ROOM — DAY

Mom sits at the table counting popsicle sticks, moving them
from one shoebox to another. Bill and Rebecca enter and sit
down. An awkward silence ensues.

                         BILL
      Hey, Mom.

                         MOM
      Wait.

She keeps counting, then stops and writes down a number.

                         MOM
      Okay. What is it?

                         BILL
      Nothing. Just thought we'd say "Hi."

                         MOM
          (pause)
      Hi.

                    BILL
We should do something together. The three
of us.

                    MOM
        (looking confused)
Okay. I suppose.
        (pause)
We could play a game.

                    REBECCA
How about poker? I'm pretty good at it.

                    MOM
No, no, no. That's a game for men. For
gamblers and reprobates.

                    BILL
        (quickly)
How about Hearts? Mom, you love playing
Hearts.

                    REBECCA
I don't know how to play that.

                    MOM
Oh, it's simple. We can teach you. Billy,
get the cards. In the china cabinet, right
behind you.

Rebecca offers a small sigh. A stressful game of Hearts ensues.

INT. BILL'S ROOM — DAY

A chair is braced against the door to make sure it stays
closed. Bill and Rebecca are lying in his bed. She's on her
stomach, naked, her head on a pillow, facing Bill. He's tracing
a tattoo at the small of her back with his finger.

                    BILL
You have nice tattoos.

                    REBECCA
You don't have any.

                    BILL
Never came up with anything I wanted to
make permanent.

                    REBECCA
Never?

                    BILL
You want to put your name on my ass?

                    REBECCA
I could carve it there with my knife.

                    BILL
You're too good to me.

                    REBECCA
Better than you deserve.

                    BILL
I like to think we deserve each other.

Rebecca lifts her head off the pillow, then rests it again,
facing away from him.

                    REBECCA
We did one thing wrong.

                    BILL
What's that?

                    REBECCA
We broke your rule. With the tower. We did
it too close. That was inside our comfort
zone. It was our own fucking backyard.

                    BILL
Don't worry. No one's going to catch us. No
one knows a thing.

She raises her body, propping on her elbows.

                    REBECCA
It's so weird. I never felt that way. Not
in my whole life. When that water hit.

                    BILL
          Yeah. It was good.

                    REBECCA
          It's like we can do anything. Like no one
          can stop us. Anything we dream up, we can
          make it real.

                    BILL
          Sure. Why not?

                    REBECCA
          Yeah.

Rebecca rests her body back down on the bed.

                    BILL
          So, Becky . . . tell me something.

                    REBECCA
          What?

                    BILL
          Now that I know almost everything about
          you, I need to know one more thing.

                    REBECCA
          Yeah? What's that?

                    BILL
          What do you want to be? When you grow up?

Rebecca lifts her head off the pillow. She pauses a moment.

                    REBECCA
          I don't know. I thought about going to
          college. I always wanted to be a teacher.
          Or a ballerina. Or a porn star.

                    BILL
          You don't have to go to college for that.

                    REBECCA
          What? They don't teach classes in
          cocksucking?

                    BILL
          You don't need classes. Hell, you could
          teach classes.

                    REBECCA
          You're so sweet.

She reaches out to hold him.

INT. BILL'S HOUSE — DAY

Mom sits at the dining room table building an elaborate art
project using toothpicks and popsicle sticks. It's an intricate
latticework that looks like it might collapse at any second.

Rebecca walks in and stares at the project. Mom keeps working,
taking no notice of Rebecca.

                    REBECCA
          Can I help? With that? Or with . . .
          anything?

                    MOM
          No, no.

                    REBECCA
          Are you sure? I feel like I should be doing
          something around here. Housework?

                    MOM
          No.

                    REBECCA
          I feel like I should be paying rent.

                    MOM
          No. My God, no. You don't owe a thing.

                    REBECCA
          But . . . I just feel . . .

                    MOM
          No. If anything, I should . . . No.
          Everything's fine. We're fine. We're all
          fine.

Rebecca looks at Mom, trying to understand her attitude. Mom
refuses to look up from her work. Rebecca finally leaves.

EXT. BILL'S HOUSE — DUSK

Bill walks around the side of the house. He sees two boys
carrying a long wooden board down the street. Bill walks up the
stairs of the front porch. He stands on the porch and closes
his eyes for a second, taking a deep breath.

He hears a sudden crack of sound and pivots, reaching in his
jacket for his gun. He sees a boy smashing the board against
the curb, repeatedly making noises that sound like gunshots.
Bill takes his hand out of his jacket and tries to relax.

INT. BILL'S HOUSE — DUSK

Rebecca is packing her duffel bag in her room. She picks up the
motorcycle mirror from the table. She's about to tuck it in
the bag, then stops herself. She puts it back on the table and
keeps packing. Bill walks in.

                    BILL
          What the hell? What are you doing?

                    REBECCA
          Nothing. I just got to find someplace else
          to live.

                    BILL
          Why? What's wrong with here?

                    REBECCA
          Your mom. She doesn't want me around. She
          doesn't like me.

                    BILL
          What? What are you talking about?

                    REBECCA
          I make her uncomfortable. Or haven't you
          noticed?

                    BILL
          She just needs to get used to you being
          here, that's all.

                         REBECCA
No, that's not it. It's like she thinks I'm
not good enough. Like I'm not right for
you.

                         BILL
She doesn't even know about . . . the two
of us. Being together.

                         REBECCA
Well, she's going to find out sooner or
later. Or are we going to sneak around for
the rest of our lives?

                         BILL
No. Of course not.

                         REBECCA
Then let's get the hell out of here. Let's
get away. There's too much shit here. Way
too much.

                         BILL
But I thought you said . . .

                         REBECCA
I don't care what I said. Let's just go. I
want out.

                         BILL
No. Let's wait. Just a little. All right?

                         REBECCA
              (crossing her arms)
I'm keeping my bag packed.

INT. BILL'S HOUSE — NIGHT

Mom sits at the dining room table working on her intricate art
project. Bill walks in and stares at her a few moments.

                         BILL
Mom, could you stop that a second? I need
to ask you something.

                    MOM
          I'd really like to finish this part.

                    BILL
          This is important.

Mom reluctantly stops her work.

                    MOM
          All right. What is it?

                    BILL
          Why don't you want Rebecca here?

                    MOM
          What? That's not true.

                    BILL
          You have a problem with her. Somehow.
          Something. I want to know what it is.

                    MOM
              (in a solemn tone)
          No. You don't.

Mom goes back to her project.

                    BILL
          I do. I really do. Tell me.

                    MOM
          No. It's not . . .

                    BILL
          Yes. This isn't negotiable. I have to know.
          Whatever it is. I'm not leaving until you
          tell me. The truth. All of it.

Mom stares at Bill for a few seconds.

                    MOM
          You really want to know?

                    BILL
          Yes. Please.

Mom closes her eyes, then draws in a breath. She stands and
retrieves a shoebox from her china cabinet. She sits back down
at the table and opens the box.

She takes out a photo and hands it to Bill. It shows a young
girl with several adults at a family picnic. Bill's mom is
pregnant in the photo.

                    MOM
          Everything seemed so simple back then.
          Almost thirty years now. It was a different
          time.

                    BILL
          Is that Rebecca?

                    MOM
          She was always running around. So full of
          life. So wild.

                    BILL
          She's cute.

                    MOM
          That was a Fourth of July. Everyone was
          there. Except you. You weren't born yet.
          You were still inside me.

                    BILL
          So why don't you like her?

                    MOM
          No, Bill, it's not that . . . no. I love
          her.
               (shaking her head)
          I never dreamed it would come to this.

                    BILL
          Come to what?

                    MOM
          Sit down.

                    BILL
          No. Just tell me.

Mom lifts a small Bible from the box and cradles the book in her hands, staring at it for a long moment.

> MOM
> Your grandfather, he was a very strict man. He always had this book with him. Just in case the Lord took him away.

> BILL
> Okay. That's nice. What does that have to do with anything?

> MOM
> Your grandfather did not approve of babies born out of wedlock.

> BILL
> Like . . . Rebecca?

> MOM
> Yes.

> BILL
> So why is that a problem now? Grandpa's been dead a long time.

Mom nods. She keeps staring at the Bible.

> BILL
> I don't get it. Jimbo wasn't married when Rebecca was born? What's the big deal?

> MOM
> No, he was married.

> BILL
> But you said . . .

> MOM
> Your father and I . . . _we_ weren't married.

> BILL
> What?

> MOM
> I was only 15.

                    BILL
        (a whisper)
What?

                    MOM
My dad . . . he decided that my baby would
be raised by Jim and Betty. They were
married and they had children already. Two
boys.

                    BILL
What the . . .

                    MOM
I had no choice. Your father ran off
because he thought my dad would kill him.
I was so happy when he came back. But by
then Rebecca was almost four years old and
I couldn't take her away from the only
parents she had known. I couldn't. It
just . . .

                    BILL
Wait. You're saying . . .

                    MOM
Rebecca is not your cousin.

                    BILL
She's my . . .

                    MOM
Sister.

                    BILL
Oh fuck.

                    MOM
I'm sorry. I should have told you long ago.
That you had . . .

                    BILL
Damn right you should have told me!

                    MOM
I thought you liked being an only child.

                    BILL
My God. I'm so screwed . . .

                    MOM
I'm sorry. Billy . . .

                    BILL
That's why it feels like we're so
connected. It's because we are. Fuck.

                    MOM
Billy. Don't use that language. It's not
the end of the world.
        (realizing)
Unless . . .

                    BILL
Yeah.

                    MOM
You're in love?

                    BILL
The one girl I want . . .

Rebecca walks in, her mouth open, her eyes watery. Mom stands
up, a stunned look on her face.

                    REBECCA
What the <u>hell</u>?

                    BILL
Oh shit.

                    REBECCA
I heard you. I heard everything. You're
my fucking brother? And you . . . you're
my <u>mother</u>? Holy Christ, I don't fucking
believe it. What the hell is this?

                    BILL
You got me.

                    MOM
I'm sorry. I'm so sorry.

                         REBECCA
My life was so fucked up by my mom. That
woman who pretended to be my mom. All that
time . . . I could have had a normal life?

                         BILL
I don't know, my life wasn't exactly
normal.

                         REBECCA
It was a damn sight better than mine. All
the shit I had to put up with. Every single
day. Jesus. I could have had a decent
mother. And you . . . you're my brother?
What the fuck?

Rebecca pounds on his back weakly.

                         BILL
I can't take this. This . . . I can't . . .

Bill leaves. Rebecca stares at Mom for a long time. Mom can't
bring herself to say anything or even look at Rebecca.

                         REBECCA
How the hell . . .

Rebecca turns and runs out of the room. Mom sits down and
stares at her art project, still intact.

EXT. BILL'S FRONT YARD — NIGHT

Rebecca catches up to Bill outside, only to find him standing
frozen. He's facing Lenny, who has a gun pointed at Bill.
They're twenty feet apart.

                         REBECCA
Don't do it, Lenny. Put the gun down.

                         LENNY
Why should I?

                         BILL
Go ahead. Pull the trigger. I don't care.
You'll be doing me a favor.

                    REBECCA
Put it down, Lenny.

                    LENNY
This is the pansyass you love?
        (pause)
Well? Answer me!

Rebecca and Bill look at each other.

                    REBECCA
No. He's just a guy. He's nothing.

                    LENNY
Really? Then you won't mind if I pump a few
bullets into his skull?

                    REBECCA
Come on. Don't be stupid. He's not worth
it.

                    LENNY
Yeah. Sure. You're lying. Tell me the
truth. Right now. He's got exactly <u>five
seconds</u> to live.

                    REBECCA
Wait! You can't! He's my brother!

                    LENNY
What? Are you kidding me? This fucker
nearly blew my head off.

                    REBECCA
We're brother and sister, I swear. We're
not in love, not like you think. That would
be sick. He was just trying to protect me.

                    LENNY
So tell me, asshole . . . you really her
brother?

                    BILL
Yeah. So what?

                        LENNY
You and her?

                        BILL
Nothing I can do about it. I'm stuck with
it forever. That sweet little girl. So
completely messed up.

                        REBECCA
Thanks.

                        BILL
        (looking at Rebecca)
Rebecca is my sister. And I love her more
than anything in the world. I will always
love her . . .
        (looking at Lenny)
even with my dying breath.

Lenny lowers his gun.

                        LENNY
That's very nice. Very touching. I'll be
glad to help you out with that.

Lenny raises his gun and fires once. Bill instantly falls to
the ground.

                        REBECCA
        (screaming)
No!

Rebecca pulls out her gun and fires three times at Lenny. He
falls, bloodied. She rushes over to Bill.

                        REBECCA
God damn it. You better not die, you
motherfucker.

                        BILL
        (sitting up)
I'm fine.

                        REBECCA
You're shot.

                        BILL
          It's only a flesh wound.
               (smiles)
          What about him?

Rebecca and Bill walk over to Lenny, lying bloodied on the
ground.

                        BILL
          Whoa. That's gotta hurt.

Bill pokes Lenny's body with his foot. Lenny groans.

                        BILL
          He's still alive.

Rebecca pushes Bill back and fires a few more rounds.

                        REBECCA
          Not anymore.

                        BILL
          Jesus.

                        REBECCA
          Let's go.

Rebecca grabs Bill and they hop on his motorcycle. Bill gives
her the keys and Rebecca fires up the engine. Bill holds her
from behind as they ride off down the street. Bill's mom comes
out on the porch and stares in disbelief.

EXT. WATERTOWER WRECKAGE SITE — NIGHT

Bill sits on the grass. Rebecca kneels next to him. The cycle
leans against a nearby tree. Yellow police tape stretches
out behind them. Rebecca tends to Bill's wound by wrapping a
bandana around his arm.

                        BILL
          Don't say anything.

                        REBECCA
          Okay.

                         BILL
          Let's never . . . say anything.

                       REBECCA
          All right.
               (pause)
          But . . .

                         BILL
          Don't. We're good.

Rebecca finishes her work with Bill's wound. Then she stares
down at the grass.

                       REBECCA
          I need to know. You and me. Is it wrong?

                         BILL
               (thinks a long moment)
          I just want to be with you.

                       REBECCA
          Yeah. You do.

Bill takes her hand.

                         BILL
          Listen to me. I love you.

Rebecca looks away. Then she looks back at Bill and grins.

                       REBECCA
          Fuck you.

Bill grins, knowing the truth.

They kiss. For a long time. For the first time.

                       THE END

Thanks for reading.

Visit www.2CloseToHome.com for more information.

The film rights are available. Please contact me at
AndradeDean@aol.com.